Becoming
Soul Mates

Resources by Les and Leslie Parrott

Books

Becoming Soul Mates
Getting Ready for the Wedding
Love Is
The Love List
The Marriage Mentor Manual
Meditations on Proverbs for Couples
Questions Couples Ask
Relationships
Relationships Workbook
Saving Your Marriage Before It Starts
Saving Your Marriage Before It Starts Workbook for Men
Saving Your Marriage Before It Starts Workbook for Women
Saving Your Second Marriage Before It Starts
Saving Your Second Marriage Before It Starts Workbook for Men
Saving Your Second Marriage Before It Starts Workbook for Women
When Bad Things Happen to Good Marriages

Video Curriculum—ZondervanGroupware™

Relationships
Saving Your Marriage Before It Starts
Mentoring Engaged and Newlywed Couples

Audio Pages®

Relationships
Saving Your Marriage Before It Starts
Saving Your Second Marriage Before It Starts
When Bad Things Happen to Good Marriages

Books by Les Parrott III

High Maintenance Relationships
Life You Want Your Kids to Live
Seven Secrets of a Healthy Dating Relationship
Once Upon a Family

Books by Leslie Parrott

If You Ever Needed Friends, It's Now
God Loves You Nose to Toes (children's book)

Becoming
Soul Mates

Cultivating

Spiritual Intimacy

in the Early Years

of Marriage

Les & Leslie Parrott

ZONDERVAN™

GRAND RAPIDS, MICHIGAN 49530

ZONDERVAN™

Becoming Soul Mates
Copyright © 1995 by Les and Leslie Parrott

Requests for information should be addressed to:

Zondervan, *Grand Rapids, Michigan 49530*

Library of Congress Cataloging-in-Publication Data

Parrott, Les.
    Becoming soul mates : cultivating spiritual intimacy in the early years of
marriage / Les Parrott III and Leslie Parrott.
       p.   cm.
    Includes bibliographical references.
    ISBN: 0–310–21926–4 (softcover)
    1. Married people—Prayer-books and devotions—English. 2. Devotional
calendars. I. Parrott, Leslie, 1964– . II. Title.
BV4596.M3P37 1995
242'.644—dc 20   95–9299
                                                          CIP

Interior design by Sue Koppenol

Printed in the United States of America

05 06 /❖ DC/ 17 16 15

To Tharon and Barbara Daniels,
true friends of ours
and the truest of soul mates to one another

CONTENTS

INTRODUCTION

Why Daily Devotions for Couples Often Fail

"It's my turn to read first!" Leslie hollered from the shower.

"No way! You read first last night," I shouted back.

"Pleeeease. Let me read the Old Testament passage first," said Leslie.

For about a week and a half—or up to the eighth chapter of Genesis, whichever came first—this exchange became routine for us. Each night we sparred with each other over who would read the Bible first during our devotional time. We had set our sights on reading the Bible clear through as a couple, and each night before we went to sleep we would take turns reading a passage from the Old Testament and then one from the New.

But after a few evenings, the focus of our lofty spiritual quest was more about sleep than Scripture. We fought over who got to read first, not because of our spiritual passion, but because that person could doze or even fall asleep while the other was reading his or her passage!

Spending a systematic, meaningful quiet time with each other, reading God's Word and praying, has never come easy for us. We have tried setting aside time in the morning. And we have tried it in the evening. Time seems to make little difference. We could never stick to it and our times were never what we hoped for. Worst of all, the problem made us feel guilty. If we were good Christians, with God at the center of our marriage, wouldn't setting aside time to cultivate spiritual intimacy be something that would come easy?

Not hardly.

We know and admire couples who open their Bibles together after breakfast, read a passage, share their secrets, and kneel to pray. But that never seemed to be our style. We wake up at different times on different days. We don't have the same routine every day. And, to be honest, we need an activity that doesn't seem like a duty that hangs over our heads.

Still, we have a restless aching, each of us, not just to know God individually, but to experience God as a couple. But how? How do we really allow God to fill the soul of our marriage?

OUR SPIRITUAL QUEST

When researchers examined the characteristics of couples who had been married for more than two decades and were fulfilled, one of the most important qualities they found was "faith in God and spiritual commitment." We never needed scientists to tell us that spiritual meaning was important to our marriage. We knew it from the start. Marriage is not a superficial bonding, a mere machine that needs routine maintenance to keep it functioning. Marriage for us is founded upon a mutual exchange of holy pledges. It is ultimately a deep, mysterious, and unfathomable spiritual endeavor.

Several years ago we started a program for engaged and newly married couples that eventually became a book and video package called *Saving Your Marriage Before It Starts*. Thousands of couples have gone through this program and for a number of years now we have formally and informally surveyed and interviewed many of them. In addition, we have interviewed many churchgoing couples who have been married for years. We wanted to learn how successful couples tend the soul of marriage.

So we asked Christian couples to measure just how important spiritual intimacy in marriage is to them, often on a ten-point scale.

And the answer was almost always the same: *very important*. Nearly every couple said they place a high value on spiritual intimacy.

But when we asked these same couples how satisfied they were with the current level of spiritual intimacy in their marriage, their answers again became predictable: *not very satisfied*. "We agree on tithing and stuff," one woman confided, "but we don't have any deep or meaningful conversations about spiritual matters." A husband told us, "I feel so uncomfortable praying with my wife. I mean she sees me seven days a week, she knows how I live!"

So, for some time now, we have been on a quest to find a means to spiritual intimacy in marriage that works—for us and the couples in our program. This book is the result. We believe it provides the tools for you and your partner to have a consistent and meaningful time together that is both enjoyable and spiritually enriching.

USING THIS BOOK FOR ALL ITS WORTH

The key to making *Becoming Soul Mates* work for you is its flexibility. There is no one right way of using it. Think of this book as a resource you mold and fit to your personal style.

Since we found that a weekly approach works best for most couples, the book provides fifty-two sessions. You may have your own personal quiet time each day, but meeting once a week as a couple is critical to becoming soul mates. Once you establish a pattern (each Sunday evening, for example), you will find that these sessions become a spiritual refueling station for the soul of your marriage.

Here's how each session is organized:

Opening Thought

Each session begins with a brief devotional thought on a marriage-relevant topic. These openings contain references to

Scripture that can be studied more in depth if you desire. You may also want to use these references for your individual study throughout the week. You may wish to read the opening devotional thought separately on your own, but we believe most couples will benefit from reading the passage aloud together.

From God's Word

The opening thought is followed by a passage of Scripture from the New International Version of the Bible that relates to the same topic. It is printed in the book to allow easy accessibility, but you may also want to read it in your own Bible to compare translations or to provide a fuller context. Either way, one of you can read the passage out loud.

Your Turn

Material for a brief time of discussion follows the Scripture reading. Several questions and suggestions encourage you to share relevant examples from your own lives. These questions and discussion starters are not meant to be completed in a hurry. The point is not to have your quiet time "checked off" your to-do list. If you are short on time, just select one or two of the questions. Don't feel that you need to answer every one every time.

Real-Life Soul Mates

The sessions also contain boxed material contributed by devoted couples who have found their own way of cultivating spiritual intimacy. These are offered as inspirational glimpses into some of the most spiritually astute couples we know. You will soon discover that every couple travels a unique route toward spiritual oneness. These real-life examples will help you and your partner chart your own course toward becoming soul mates.

Soul to Soul

We have found that busy couples who are motivated to deepen their spiritual intimacy throughout a hectic week need to intentionally address three things: (1) what they gained as a couple from their session together; (2) what their partner is facing in the coming week that they will remember in their personal prayers; and (3) what they can do in a concrete way that will communicate kindness toward their partner in the coming week.

By addressing these three concerns *each week*, partners strengthen and deepen their soul-to-soul connection. They build a loving marriage bond of mutual appreciation and respect that is irreversible.

We call this part of your session "soul to soul," and it is at the heart of your quiet time together. To insure that you are understanding your partner's soul and that you will remember his or her concerns in prayer, and that you will make a conscious plan for meeting his or her needs in the upcoming week, we recommend that you take notes. *Write down what you gained from your time together, what your partner's need is, and what you will do to increase the odds of him or her having a better upcoming week.*

Prayer

Concluding each session is a printed prayer. Prayer is vital to healthy marriages but sometimes tough for married couples to do together. So we offer a simple prayer at the end of each session for you to read aloud or quietly by yourselves. We hope that these brief prayers will be a catalyst for the prayers of your heart.

OTHER WAYS OF BENEFITING FROM *BECOMING SOUL MATES*

The most obvious way of using *Becoming Soul Mates* is to proceed from the first session to the last, week by week. But this is not necessary. You may choose to peruse the table of contents and turn selectively to the theme that seems relevant to you for that specific week. Feel free to choose session themes in the order that addresses your needs.

You might also consider using *Becoming Soul Mates* with a small group or in a Sunday school class for couples. For example, someone in the group could read aloud the Scripture passage and the opening thought. The group may even want to provide time for one-on-one discussion for couples and then reconvene for a lesson, an activity, or a group discussion.

Your marriage relationship will either develop a depth that binds your two souls together, or it will experience a superficial bonding which rides the waves of emotion until the relationship is beached for lack of depth. So we offer a prayer for you. The yearning you and your partner have to be connected soul to soul can only be satisfied when your spirits are intertwined with a greater Spirit, Jesus Christ. So as you use the tool of *Becoming Soul Mates*, we pray that God's Son will dwell in your relationship richly.

Les & Leslie Parrott
Seattle, Washington

LIVING HAPPILY EVER AFTER

The first apartment we had was so small that our prized possession, a hand-me-down king-sized bed with a matching chest of drawers and big-framed mirror, had to be put in the living area. The kitchen was so small it would only accommodate one of us at a time. The walls were so thin they were little more than a sight barrier to our neighbor, whose conversations could sometimes be monitored.

That was then, this is now. After ten years in one-bedroom apartments we now have our own house. It has a well-proportioned bedroom that holds our big bed and all the matching pieces. Our kitchen includes a cooking island large enough for both of us to prepare the food or clean the mess together. And the sounds of neighbors are too far away to matter.

So has it made a difference in our marriage? Are we happier now that we have accumulated more "stuff," or were we just as happy when we had next to nothing? In some ways we are happier now, or at least more relaxed. We no longer post the monthly income in twenty-dollar bills on the wall above the kitchen sink and visibly watch and pray for a twenty to be left over at the end of the month for some discretionary spending. We both work and we don't spend all we make. And to that extent, we are happier because of reduced financial anxiety.

But at this point in the maturation of our marriage, we've come to realize more and more that it is our relationship with each other that matters most, not the comfort and conveniences we have around us. No matter how much a couple has, they always believe a little bit more would be just enough. In fact, studies have shown that most couples believe they would be happier if their income were twenty percent higher. Of course, twenty percent more will never satisfy, at least not for long. As our increases are absorbed into the living standard, expectations rise and the cycle repeats itself.

Above a certain subsistence level which varies with the life stage of each couple, happiness and marriage depend on the quality of the relationship. And this is true at all stages of life, for richer, for poorer. The writer of Ecclesiastes says, "Better one handful with tranquillity than two handfuls with toil and chasing after the wind" (Eccl. 4:6; see also Prov. 15:17; 17:1).

So if you are living in a one-bedroom apartment praying that your monthly income will outlast the month, remember these wise words: "Do not wear yourself out to get rich; have the wisdom to show restraint. Cast but a glance at riches, and they are gone, for they will surely sprout wings and fly off to the sky like an eagle" (Prov. 23:4–5). It is far more rewarding to work at becoming soul mates. For the riches of a happy marriage will outlast all other possessions.

FROM GOD'S WORD

Command those who are rich in this present world not to be arrogant nor to put their hope in wealth, which is so uncertain, but to put their hope in God, who richly provides us with everything for our enjoyment. Command them to do good, to be rich in good deeds, and to be generous and willing to share. In this way they will lay up treasure for themselves as a firm foundation for the coming age, so that they may take hold of the life that is truly life.

1 TIMOTHY 6:17–19

REAL-LIFE SOUL MATES

A couple we knew gave us some advice several months before we married twenty-three years ago. That advice has served us well and upon reflection is one of the main ways we have cultivated spiritual intimacy in our relationship.

Our friends introduced us to the "principle of rein-troduction." Simply put, this principle acknowledges that every day we change as individuals based on our experiences that day. In order to build a growing relationship as a couple, then, we must make time to "daily reintroduce" ourselves to each other. We share the mundane and the profound. We disclose what's going on in our own lives and genuinely inquire about each other's life.

Frankly, this was fairly easy to do when we were first married and had few distractions. We had lots of time for meaningful dialogue, cups of coffee, and sharing activities together. But as children came and other adult responsibilities began to crowd our schedules, we were grateful we had established this habit early on and that it still prevails. For no amount of reading the Bible or praying together genuinely builds our relationship if we haven't bared our lives with each other on a regular basis and feel convinced that we are "naked and unashamed" with each other in the fullest sense of that biblical definition of intimacy.

Now our daily reintroduction habit usually takes the form of a long walk, an extended cup of coffee (decaf, now), or a long phone call if I'm out of town. But we keep very short accounts, and we can testify that we depend on this habit to keep us growing, both as individuals and as a couple.

SCOTT AND JILL BOLINDER

❧ Your Turn

- Why would the passage from 1 Timothy warn against putting your hope in wealth? How does being "rich in good deeds" apply to marriage?
- Give an example of a time when you experienced peace and contentment in your marriage even in the absence of creature comforts. What made it so?
- If you are like most couples, you probably believe a little more income would make you a lot more happy. What kinds of differences do you think you would notice?
- Do you agree with the writer of Ecclesiastes that "better [is] one handful with tranquillity than two … with toil"? If so, how are you applying that to your marriage relationship?
- In what practical ways are you investing in your marriage so that it will outlast material possessions?

❧ Soul to Soul

To deepen your spiritual intimacy this next week, make note of:

- What you gained from this session together.
- A pressure point in your partner's upcoming week you will pray about.
- A concrete kindness you can offer your partner this week.

❧ Prayer

Gracious God, thank you for our marriage. Thank you for the joy and happiness it brings to our lives. Teach us to realize that drawing our strength from you and learning to love one another is critical to our well-being. We long to be soul mates and ask you to teach us how. Amen.

❧

Session Two:
Double Your Serve

Dietrich Bonhoeffer, the German theologian who was hanged by the Nazis during World War II, wrote a wonderful wedding sermon while he was in prison, but he never had a chance to deliver it in person. He wrote:

> Marriage is more than your love for each other. It has a higher dignity and power, for it is God's holy ordinance. . . . In your love you see only the heaven of your happiness, but in marriage you are placed at a post of responsibility toward the world and mankind. Your love is your own private possession, but marriage is something more than personal—it is a status, an office . . . that joins you together in the sight of God.

Have you thought about the "higher dignity and power" of your marriage? We know of nothing else that can cultivate the intimacy of soul mates more than reaching out to the world as a team. Doing good for others as a couple brings a mystical quality into your marriage. It helps you transcend yourselves and become part of something larger.

God is committed to one major objective: helping us conform to the image of his Son (see Phil. 2:5–11). And his Son, Scripture says, came not to be served but to serve (Mark 10:45). It is as straightforward as that. God wants us to be a giving people. Philippians 2:4 says, "Look not only to your own interests, but also to the interests of others." Galatians 5:13 says, "Serve one another in love."

Marriage is a great means to becoming more like Christ. Paul says to "spur one another on toward love and good deeds" (Heb. 10:24). Marriage helps us do just that, and when we join our efforts in service together we are doubly blessed.

There are literally hundreds of ways to incorporate shared service into your marriage—offering hospitality in your home, volunteering at a shelter, sponsoring a needy child, working in the church nursery. The key is to find something that fits your personal style. One of the ways we enjoy reaching out as a couple is by doing something anonymously. Even something small. We call it a mission of service in secret. It is an act of kindness that is concealed from everyone but the two of us. Our own sense of devotion and intimacy deepens as we secretly observe the results of our service.

Two people joined in marriage, as Bonhoeffer said, are ordained to serve others as a team. As a partnership, two people can serve other people better than they could as separate individuals. So don't neglect the practice of shared service. It will do more to enrich the soul of your marriage than you can ever imagine.

FROM GOD'S WORD

Whoever wants to become great among you must be your servant, and whoever wants to be first must be slave of all. For even the Son of Man did not come to be served, but to serve, and to give his life as a ransom for many.

MARK 10:43–45 ❧

REAL-LIFE SOUL MATES

We fell in love in 1983 while working with the homeless in the nutty, wonderful neighborhood of Haight-Ashbury in San Francisco. A couple of years passed before we admitted that we were two pilgrims on the same path of life and ministry. We wanted to be together wherever life and our shared callings might take us, so in 1985 we married.

During the first decade of our marriage we traveled to exotic places, from Calcutta, working at Mother Teresa's Home for the Dying, to Minsk, bringing medical supplies for the children made ill by the Chernobyl nuclear disaster. Our home is cluttered with boxes of photographs and our bookshelves are full of "treasures" from faraway places. We love to show and tell the tales behind these mementos. We laugh when we see ourselves sweaty and bleary-eyed from India's sweltering heat or bundled up in layer upon layer to ward off January's cold in Belarus. And then we talk of the people we met—those with whom we've feasted, laughed, cried, and prayed. Our "family" photos include people from vastly different cultures. Our adventures in ministry have given us an extended family that spans the globe.

We have a photograph in our dining room of a long banquet table set for a feast. Appearing to stretch into eternity, it reminds us that one day we shall feast with all of the faithful—the many we know worldwide and the multitudes we have not yet met. In anticipation of that day, we imagine sitting next to each other so we can elbow one another and say, "Hey, isn't that Vladimir? Look, there's Carolita. What do you know, Carl finally made it after all. Thanks be to God."

MICHAEL CHRISTENSEN AND REBECCA LAIRD

❧ Your Turn

- What role does shared service play in your spiritual journey together? Are you reaching out as a team the way you would like to?
- Give an example of how your partner has inspired you to do a specific good deed.
- In your opinion, how is intimacy in marriage linked to shared service?
- Bonhoeffer said that shared service gives your marriage "dignity and meaning." What does that mean to you?
- How can the two of you more effectively practice shared service in your marriage? What specific things might you do?

❧ Soul to Soul

To deepen your spiritual intimacy this next week, make note of:

- What you gained from this session together.
- A pressure point in your partner's upcoming week you will pray about.
- A concrete kindness you can offer your partner this week.

❧ Prayer

Dear God, reveal to us the higher dignity and power of our marriage. Teach us to spur one another on, gently and lovingly, toward becoming more like Christ. We want to double our efforts by serving you together as a team, so please help us discover our unique gift of shared service as a couple. We pray this sincerely. Amen.

Session Three:
All for a Bar of Soap

In *Love in the Time of Cholera*, Nobel laureate Gabriel García Márquez portrays a marriage that disintegrates over a bar of soap. It was the wife's job to keep the house in order, including the towels, toilet paper, and soap in the bathroom. One day she forgot to replace the soap. Her husband exaggerated the oversight: "I've been bathing for almost a week without any soap." She vigorously denied forgetting to replace the soap. Although she had indeed forgotten, her pride was at stake, and she would not back down. For the next seven months they slept in separate rooms and ate in silence. Their marriage had suffered a heart attack.

"Even when they were old and placid," writes Márquez, "they were very careful about bringing it up, for the barely healed wounds could begin to bleed again as if they had been inflicted only yesterday." How can a bar of soap ruin a marriage? The answer is actually simple: Neither partner would say, "Forgive me."

Forgiveness is critically important to the success of marriage. In becoming soul mates you must wrap and rewrap your partnership over and over with many layers of forgiveness. Why, you ask? Because forgiveness is the only way to break the inevitable cycle of blame and pain in a marriage. Two people living together are going to, at some point, get on each other's nerves. A power struggle will emerge over a tit-for-tat issue: "I can't believe you didn't buy the cereal I like."

"Wait a minute, aren't you supposed to be in charge of the groceries?"

"Don't try to pass the blame to me—you said you would buy it."

"Yes, but I told you to remind me."

"Why should I? It's your responsibility."

Such inane conversation bleats on and on in marriage until one of the partners says, "I'm sorry. Will you forgive me?" Marriage cannot last without forgiveness. If you are looking for fairness, don't look for it in marriage. Soul mates survive on forgiveness, not fairness.

Forgiving your partner is a way of saying, "I'm human. I make mistakes. I want to be granted that privilege, and so I grant you that privilege." The fourth chapter of Hebrews makes explicit this mystery of incarnation on a higher level: "We do not have a high priest who is unable to sympathize with our weaknesses, but we have one who has been tempted in every way, just as we are—yet was without sin" (verse 15).

Charles Williams has suggested that "no word in English carries a greater possibility of terror than the little word *as* in 'forgive us our trespasses, as we forgive those who trespass against us.' For this clause in the Lord's Prayer tells us that 'the condition of forgiving then is to be forgiven; the condition of being forgiven is to forgive.'"

So wrap your marriage in forgiveness. "Be kind and compassionate to one another, forgiving each other, just as in Christ God forgave you" (Eph. 4:32).

FROM GOD'S WORD

Therefore, as God's chosen people, holy and dearly loved, clothe yourselves with compassion, kindness, humility, gentleness and patience. Bear with each other and forgive whatever grievances you may have against one another. Forgive as the Lord forgave you. And over all these virtues put on love, which binds them all together in perfect unity.

COLOSSIANS 3:12–14 ❧

REAL-LIFE SOUL MATES

Heidi and I realized early in our marriage that a prerequisite to intimacy of any kind was a foundation of respect for each other and for our relationship. As a result we've tried to build and maintain what I've since referred to as a "Wall of Tenderness" designed to keep out destructive attitudes, while keeping us close to each other. This wall entails:

- Not discussing problems in harsh, angry tones, but in attentive conversation, while working toward solutions that genuinely satisfy both of us.
- Not joking cuttingly about each other, especially in front of others.
- Never kidding about divorce.
- Saving constructive criticism for when we're alone and in a receptive frame of mind.
- Being willing to give in to each other's preferences, and developing a language for conveying when that is really needed. Some friends encouraged us to reserve the simple phrase "this is really important to me" for those times when we most need to be heard and respected.
- Regularly giving verbal and nonverbal encouragement to each other for who we are as well as for what we do. This includes doing things that make the other person feel treasured, including dinner dates, gifts, messages, prayers, and time alone together without distractions.
- Fostering an attitude that says, in effect, "I'd rather die than hurt or bring shame on you. You're the one precious person to whom I've committed my love for the rest of my life."

These actions and attitudes have helped us to build a strong foundation for our marriage. We're thankful to say that after almost twelve years together, we're still in love, still laughing together, still learning and growing together. And we're looking forward with anticipation to the next twelve years.

MARK AND HEIDI MITTELBERG

❧ Your Turn

- Discuss the meaning of Christ's message about forgiveness in the Lord's Prayer and how it relates to your marriage.
- Give an example of a time when forgiveness broke the cycle of blame and pain in your marriage.
- Sometimes it is as difficult to ask for forgiveness as it is to grant it. How can each of you work on taking the initiative in this?
- Have you ever fallen into the trap of believing marriage is supposed to be fair? What allows you to make a shift from fairness to forgiveness in your marriage?
- What is one thing you can do to prepare in advance to face the next unfair situation with repentance and forgiveness between you?

❧ Soul to Soul

To deepen your spiritual intimacy this next week, make note of:

- What you gained from this session together.
- A pressure point in your partner's upcoming week you will pray about.
- A concrete kindness you can offer your partner this week.

❧ Prayer

Lord, save us from making major issues out of minor incidents. Teach us how to distinguish what is significant and what is not. Also, teach us to walk the path of forgiveness in our marriage. Weave repentance and forgiveness into the fabric of our marriage by your grace. Amen.

Session Four:
Lighten Up

We laugh a lot together. Not a day goes by, it seems, that one of us does not crack up the other one—on purpose or by accident. An unexpected expression, a mispronounced word, or a faux pas in front of others is all it takes to get us laughing. A line from a movie or sitcom that struck us funny will be repeated in our home for weeks. But every once in a while, usually in the midst of an intense and serious talk when one of us is not yet ready to play, a joke will backfire.

Humor is always risky. What is appealing to some is appalling to others. In a survey of over fourteen thousand *Psychology Today* readers who rated thirty jokes, the findings were unequivocal. "Every single joke," it was reported, "had a substantial number of fans who rated it 'very funny,' while another group dismissed it as 'not at all funny.'" Apparently, our funny bones are located in different places. Some laugh uproariously at the slapstick of Larry, Moe, and Curly, while others enjoy the more cerebral humor of Woody Allen.

We can't tell you exactly how to bring more laughter into your marriage; that's a matter of personal preference. But we can tell you that your marriage will benefit greatly from humor. Laughter has important physiological effects on you and your partner. The French philosopher Voltaire wrote, "The art of medicine consists of amusing the patient while nature cures the disease." Modern research indicates that people with a sense of humor have fewer symptoms of physical illness than those who are less humorous. This idea, however, is not new. Since King Solomon's time, people have known about and applied the healing benefits of humor. Proverbs 17:22 tells us, "A cheerful heart is good medicine."

In fact, the Bible as a whole reminds us again and again of the "sounds of joy and gladness" (Jer. 7:34). The book of Proverbs says that "the cheerful heart has a continual feast" (15:15). The psalmist sings, "Our mouths were filled with laughter" (126:2). Isaiah exults, "Shout for joy, O heavens; rejoice, O earth" (49:13). Jesus told his disciples that after he left them, "your grief will turn to joy . . . and no one will take away your joy" (John 16:20, 22). The apostle Peter confirms that the Christians to whom he is writing "are filled with an inexpressible and glorious joy" (1 Peter 1:8).

Humor helps us cope—not just with the trivial but even with the tragic. Martin Grotjahn, author of *Beyond Laughter*, notes that "to have a sense of humor is to have an understanding of human suffering." Charlie Chaplin could have said the same thing. Chaplin grew up in the poorest section of London. His mother suffered from serious mental illness and his father died of alcoholism when Charlie was just five. Laughter was Chaplin's tool for coping with life's losses.

"If you can find humor in anything," according to Bill Cosby, "you can survive it." Researchers agree. Studies reveal that individuals who have a strong sense of humor are less likely to experience depression and other forms of mood disturbance.

So it is not surprising that humor is good for your marriage. To paraphrase the nineteenth-century minister Henry Ward Beecher, a marriage without a sense of humor is like a wagon without springs—jolted by every bump in the road. Do your marriage a favor. Smooth out the bumpy times with a little laughter.

REAL-LIFE SOUL MATES

We decided early in our marriage to establish a regularly scheduled "date night"! Just the two of us, alone. To laugh, to lift our spirits, to love. How stimulating and interesting these nights are to both of us! It puts the two of us more at ease with each other during the remainder of the week.

It's hard to imagine what our marriage would be like today if we had not had our weekly date night. There have been precious times of quietly holding hands and looking long into each other's eyes. Because we are changing persons in a changing world, we are constantly becoming reacquainted with each other. As a result, we have grown together—not apart—as the years have passed. Yes, there are times when one of us is very fatigued, but then he or she draws energy from the other. Sometimes we even become bored with each other; then we realize that we need to be stimulated by either a change of scenery or entertainment of some kind, but ninety-five percent of the time, we want to just be together to cherish our talking and touching.

We enjoy each other more as the years go by, and because we share the same deep spiritual faith, our oneness transcends the physical. How blessed are those who experience the priceless discovery of love transcending all boundaries, all social, intellectual, physical, and spiritual limits!

ROBERT AND ARVELLA SCHULLER

FROM GOD'S WORD

Shout for joy to the LORD, all the earth. Worship the LORD with gladness; come before him with joyful songs.

PSALM 100:1 ❧

Rejoice in the Lord always. I will say it again: Rejoice!

PHILIPPIANS 4:4 ❧

❧ Your Turn

- Jesus was accused by some of enjoying life too much! In your opinion, how does his life model humor and fun?
- What things make you laugh together? How is your sense of humor similar to or different from your partner's?
- Does your humor as a couple ever turn hurtful? If so, when are those times and how can they be prevented?
- Give an example of a time when your partner's sense of humor lifted you out of a dark mood or a worried frame of mind.
- What can you do this week to lighten up as a couple?

❧ Soul to Soul

To deepen your spiritual intimacy this next week, make note of:

- What you gained from this session together.
- A pressure point in your partner's upcoming week you will pray about.
- A concrete kindness you can offer your partner this week.

❧ Prayer

Gracious God, we thank you for the healing gift of laughter and ask you to help us to laugh together often. Teach us to see ourselves in the light of eternity and laugh at what might otherwise bring worry or self-reproach. Fill us with your joy and bind us together with cheerful hearts. Amen.

Session Five:
Your Money Matters

"Why do you always make the money decisions?" I asked.

Les and I were standing in the middle of a department store trying to choose a new couch for our apartment. And it seemed to me that he was controlling the purse strings.

"I don't make the money decisions," he said, "our bank account does." That remark was followed by a lengthy, whiny discussion—okay, it was a fight—over how we manage, or should manage, our money. Was he in charge or were we in charge? Some of our biggest fights are financially focused.

Money, of course, has always provided plenty of fodder for marital discord. It is, after all, the most common source of conflict between couples. And with good reason. The dollar serves as a weapon of independence. It provides a battleground for disputes over responsibility and judgment. Financial issues can even be a forum for airing doubts about self-worth. A partner who is financially irresponsible, for example, may be broadcasting a message: Rescue me, solve my problems. A spouse's reluctance to accept gifts may hide a deeper lack of trust. A woman who goes on a spending spree every time her husband becomes cold and withdrawn may be trying to get his attention.

When money problems regularly erupt into shouting matches or hurt feelings, it may be time to seek professional help. But if you are simply trying to avoid the embarrassment of raising your voice in a furniture store, here are some suggestions from experts for trying to work things out on your own. First, educate your spouse about your own money upbringing. Talk over financial matters regularly, at a time when money decisions are not pressing. And if one person pays the bills, he or she should tell the other partner where their money is going and when. And finally, agree on and write down your financial goals, short-term and long-term.

It is hard for most couples to talk about money. Yet Jesus spoke about money more frequently than any other subject except the kingdom of God. His careful attention to financial issues is one of the truly amazing things about the Gospel narratives. The range of his concern is startling: from the parable of the sower (Matt. 13:22) to the parable of the rich farmer (Luke 12:16–21), from the encounter with the rich young ruler (Matt. 19:21) to the encounter with Zacchaeus (Luke 19), from teachings on trust in the sixth chapter of Matthew to teachings on the danger of wealth in the sixth chapter of Luke.

Behind money are invisible spiritual powers, powers that seduce and deceive. Paul saw this fact when he observed that "the love of money is a root of all kinds of evils" (1 Tim. 6:10). Every marriage must build a fortress against these beguiling forces.

From God's Word

Do not store up for yourselves treasures on earth, where moth and rust destroy, and where thieves break in and steal. But store up for yourselves treasures in heaven, where moth and rust do not destroy, and where thieves do not break in and steal. For where your treasure is, there your heart will be also.

MATTHEW 6:19–21

REAL-LIFE SOUL MATES

As life circumstances have changed throughout our twenty-five years of marriage, we have tried many ways to develop spiritual intimacy.

In the past, we've read the Bible together, discussed what we've read, and taken prayer walks (each on a different side of the street, coming together to unite periodically over a common concern). We've gone on marriage retreats and participated in marriage enrichment groups through the church. We have always spent a lot of time together.

Children added a new dimension to our spiritual intimacy. Rather than thinking of children as an interruption to our intimate times, we've learned to see them as an addition. We've read nightly devotions to the children and acted out thousands of Bible stories complete with strange accents and ad lib dialogue. We see our primary task as parents to help each family member draw closer to Jesus.

Now that our four children are all adolescents, we entertain our children less and share, discuss, and pray together more. As a couple, we colead a marriage group for young couples, which keeps us reflecting on marriage in the context of our faith. We also write love notes that often include appreciation of our partner's prayers and faith. Focusing on what we appreciate in each other builds up our partner and keeps us growing in love. We also have devotions together. We found years ago that the early morning hours held the fewest distractions. We get up at 5:30 A.M. and have individual devotions. If either needs prayer, we ask for it.

Marriage is ever-changing. We encounter new life situations and we adapt. It shouldn't be surprising, then, to realize that the ways that we are spiritually intimate with each other and with the Lord are new every morning.

KIRBY AND EV WORTHINGTON

❧ Your Turn

- Discuss the meaning of Christ's message about money from this passage in Matthew and how it relates to Paul's warning against the love of money?
- Give an example from your upbringing that illustrates your attitude toward money management.
- What are the financial goals you share as a couple and how are you working to meet them?
- Most marriages have a "spender" and "keeper." Talk about your roles and how each of you can learn from the other.
- How can the two of you prepare in advance to make your next money conflict less troublesome?

❧ Soul to Soul

To deepen your spiritual intimacy this next week, make note of:

- What you gained from this session together.
- A pressure point in your partner's upcoming week you will pray about.
- A concrete kindness you can offer your partner this week.

❧ Prayer

Loving God, help us to keep money in perspective. While it often seems we do not have enough, save us from taking our financial frustrations out on each other. And guide us in every financial decision. Help us be mature and responsible with the resources you have provided us. Amen.

Session Six:
In the Beginning ... God Created Sex!

So, how's your sex life? That's a fair question, isn't it? After all, sexuality is not a given, something that somehow miraculously takes care of itself once we enter marriage. It needs nurture, tenderness, education, and—are you ready for this—religion.

It's a fact. Religion, according to some studies, is good for your sex life. As strange as it may sound, there is a strong link in marriage between spirituality and sexuality. Married couples who cultivate spiritual intimacy are far more likely to report higher satisfaction with their sex life than other couples.

This fact makes sense if you think about it. The mysteries, wonders, and pleasures of sex in marriage are a divine gift to celebrate. Scripture—right from the beginning—enthusiastically affirms sex within the bonds of marriage.

Start with the first chapter of the Bible. It contains a magnificent comment on the meaning of sexuality in marriage. As God is bringing the universe into existence we are told that the human creation is set apart from all others, for it is the *imago Dei,* the image of God: "So God created man in his own image, in the image of God he created him; male and female he created them" (Gen. 1:27). Our maleness and femaleness is not just an accidental arrangement of the human species. Our male and female sexuality is related to our creation in the image of God. This point is echoed throughout Scripture.

Consider the Song of Songs. Karl Barth has called the Song an expanded commentary upon Genesis 2:25—"The man and his wife were both naked, and they felt no shame." If Genesis affirms our sexuality, the Song of Songs celebrates it. There is no other portion of Scripture that is more extravagant. The Song of Songs describes sensuality without licentiousness, passion without promiscuity, love without lust.

In the New Testament, Paul quotes the Genesis passage about the husband leaving father and mother and cleaving to his wife so that the two become one flesh, and then he adds: "This is a profound mystery—but I am talking about Christ and the church" (Eph. 5:32).

Jesus, likewise, underscores a high view of sex in marriage. He refers to the Genesis passage and then adds, "So they are no longer two, but one. Therefore what God has joined together, let man not separate" (Matt. 19:6).

The Old Testament and the New Testament, the Gospels and the Epistles call us to celebrate sexuality in marriage. There is no denying that your spiritual growth helps to enhance your sexual intimacy in marriage. So, we'll ask it again. How's your sex life?

From God's Word

Then the LORD God made a woman from the rib he had taken out of the man, and he brought her to the man. Then the man said, "This is now bone of my bones and flesh of my flesh; she shall be called 'woman,' for she was taken out of man." For this reason a man will leave his father and mother and be united to his wife, and they will become one flesh. The man and his wife were both naked, and they felt no shame.

GENESIS 2:22–25 ❦

REAL-LIFE SOUL MATES

We are convinced that our spiritual intimacy is a reflection of the love we share. Whether it is taking a walk, holding hands in front of the fire, or talking about God's movement in our lives, our relational commitment and intimacy is at the heart of who we are as individuals called to marriage. Though sometimes we wander off from each other, our journey in friendship and respect over the last fifteen years has deepened our experience of life in Christ as a couple.

We have few "spiritual" rituals, unless you can call a commitment to weekly dates, quarterly getaways, and spontaneous romantic interludes "spiritual rituals." We do pray together, but our prayer life is more of an extension of the intimacy we share rather than an ordered, systematic formula. We often discuss Scripture, but instead of feeling forced, it comes from the passion of God's presence and conviction of God's prompting in our lives.

This is spiritual intimacy in marriage—two children on a walk through life, each holding the hand of the One that walks with them, savoring his companionship along the way.

CHAP AND DEE CLARK

❧ Your Turn

- Discuss the link between spirituality and sexuality. How would each of you articulate this connection? How could your sex life be a barometer of your spiritual health as a couple?
- Give an example from your early years that illustrates how you were educated about sex.
- One place in marriage where we want to keep the mystery, the excitement, the fascination is in sexual intimacy. Talk about what you could do as a couple to avoid falling into a boring routine.
- Talk about how the two of you initiate sexual intimacy in your marriage. How could your times of lovemaking be better for each of you?
- How could the two of you more effectively celebrate the gift of sex in marriage?

❧ Soul to Soul

To deepen your spiritual intimacy this next week, make note of:

- What you gained from this session together.
- A pressure point in your partner's upcoming week you will pray about.
- A concrete kindness you can offer your partner this week.

❧ Prayer

Gracious God, you have enthusiastically affirmed the gift of our shared sexuality and have created us with an unfathomable capacity for intimacy and pleasure. Dwell in our marriage—enhance our oneness in body and soul. Amen.

❧

SESSION SEVEN:
CARING ENOUGH TO COMMIT

"It is easier in these United States to walk away from a marriage than from a commitment to purchase a used car," said an attorney at a conference we attended. "Most contracts cannot be unilaterally terminated. A marriage commitment, however, can be broken by practically anyone at any time, and without cause."

He is right. A friend of ours who went to traffic court heard two divorce decrees from the judge before his turn came to be heard. He dropped by our office later to tell us about his experience. He said, "I told my wife when I got home that we could have had a divorce any number of times if those reasons I heard in court were good enough for a legal separation."

A few decades back this wasn't so. In those days many had to travel to Mexico or acquire residency in Nevada in order to obtain a divorce. Others had to make believe that one of the parties had engaged in a nefarious affair. Contemporary America concluded that marital bonds were tied too tightly and responded with no-fault divorce. A generation later, the value of marriage has dwindled significantly.

The "till death do us part" of marriage, however, is not an ideal. It is a reality that is insured by an unswerving commitment—a willful agreement to keep love alive. "Do two walk together unless they have agreed to do so?" asked the prophet Amos (3:3). Commitment is the cerebral part of love. It is the part that comes more from our mind than our heart.

Why do so many marriage commitments fall flat these days? We believe it is because too many promises are made without the promises of God. We can "hold unswervingly to the hope we profess, for he who promised is faithful" (Heb. 10:23). Our commitment to each other in marriage is sustained by God's model of faithfulness to us. When a man and woman covenant with one another, God promises faithfulness to them (see 1 Cor. 1:9). There is no way to overemphasize the centrality of commitment in God's character. It is woven into every part of the Bible—from Genesis, where God initiates his promise of faithfulness, through Revelation, where John's vision depicts "a white horse, whose rider is called Faithful and True" (19:11).

Today's covenant, embodied in our partner, makes a home for our restless hearts. It accepts our whole soul by saying, "I believe in you and commit myself to you through thick and thin." Without commitment and the trust it engenders, marriage would have no hope of enduring. For no couple can achieve deep confidence in their own fidelity until they first recognize God's faithfulness to them.

FROM GOD'S WORD

Know therefore that the LORD your God is God; he is the faithful God, keeping his covenant of love to a thousand generations of those who love him and keep his commands.

DEUTERONOMY 7:9 ❧

❧ Your Turn

- Commitment is essential to knowing who God is. How would you describe this quality of God to a person who does not know him? What biblical examples and personal experiences would you use to illustrate God's commitment?
- Give an example of how God's commitment to you has been realized in your life.

REAL-LIFE SOUL MATES

I'm OK, You're OK is not a good devotional book for couples. The health of our spiritual lives rests on the recognition that we are not okay, that we are broken people in need of God's grace and healing. The Bible is replete with examples of broken, needy people who find comfort and rest, not by trusting themselves more, but by falling on their knees before God. It is a familiar pattern: Our stubborn independence is shattered by life's troubles, and God reaches us in the midst of our need.

By emulating this same pattern we cultivate spiritual intimacy in our marriage. First, we try to develop an attitude of *interdependence* by disclosing our needs and struggles to one another. Independence is the "great lie of the universe." Our marriage is strongest when we discard our myths of self-sufficiency and admit our need for one another and for God.

Second, we work to cultivate *trust* by listening non-reactively. When disclosure brings judgment and criticism or trite reassurance, people stop talking. When we allow ourselves to enter into the other's pain, to understand and empathize, then we build intimacy.

Third, we seek *humility* through the spiritual disciplines. Regularly and honestly admitting our needs to God in times of prayer and solitude encourages us to also admit our needs to each other. Encountering God's grace and forgiveness through corporate worship and personal Scripture reading inclines us to understand and forgive one another. Giving time or money to those in crisis reminds us that we are vulnerable people in need of close, helping relationships.

Spiritual intimacy in our marriage allows us to remember that we are not okay, that we are drawn into community with God only through grace, and that God provides marriage as a living metaphor of that grace.

MARK AND LISA MCMINN

- Some people are pessimistic about lifelong marriage. They have seen too many marriages fail. What makes you believe your marriage will be "till death do us part"?
- Commitment stems from a conscious decision. What are you doing to reaffirm this decision in your marriage? How is your commitment expressed?
- If someone were observing your marriage for signs of commitment, what would they take note of?

❧ Soul to Soul

To deepen your spiritual intimacy this next week, make note of:

- What you gained from this session together.
- A pressure point in your partner's upcoming week you will pray about.
- A concrete kindness you can offer your partner this week.

❧ Prayer

Gracious God, we thank you for the privilege of entering this lifelong pilgrimage of marriage together. We know that it is only through commitment that our relationship will be sustained, so we ask you to strengthen our commitment daily. And help us to express our commitment that we might be buoyed by one another's holy pledge. Amen.

❧

SESSION EIGHT:
TURNING "ME" TO "WE"

In the center of your head is a structure of the brain whose purpose is survival. It is the intensive care unit of the nervous system, the part of the supersystem that helps you stay well. Medical students remember the functions of this part of the brain, called the limbic system, by knowing that it is consumed with either fighting, fleeing, or feeding. Body temperature, heartbeat, breathing, sweating, and the general response of the body to the world begin here.

The limbic system reacts to any change in our internal or external world, a type of biological Geiger counter. But it does not read, consider, evaluate, or assess in terms of the welfare of the world. It is only concerned with survival. Unless told otherwise, there is no "us" in the lower levels of the brain, only "self."

In 2 Timothy 3:2, Paul came up with a frightening list describing the self-centered person: "People will be lovers of themselves, lovers of money, boastful, proud, abusive, disobedient to their parents, ungrateful, unholy, without love, unforgiving, slanderous, without self-control, brutal, not lovers of the good, treacherous, rash, conceited, lovers of pleasure rather than lovers of God."

None of us could abide marriage with the person described by Paul. In fact, there are laws to protect us from such persons. But according to Galatians 5:22, no law can bring about the qualities that transcend a selfish focus on "me." These qualities are the fruit of inviting the Holy Spirit to transform our self-centered tendencies. They include: love, goodness, joy, faithfulness, peace, gentleness, patience, self-control, kindness.

What person would not like to make a home with the partner who demonstrates these qualities. These are the marks of the individual who has transcended selfishness and turned "me" into "we." Every marriage runs the risk of becoming two self-centered persons consumed, like the limbic system, with individual survival. But when the Holy Spirit is allowed to transform our self-gratifying nature, the real miracle of marriage occurs: The more we give of ourselves, the more fruit we enjoy.

From God's Word

The entire law is summed up in a single command: "Love your neighbor as yourself." If you keep on biting and devouring each other, watch out or you will be destroyed by each other. So I say, live by the Spirit, and you will not gratify the desires of the sinful nature. For the sinful nature desires what is contrary to the Spirit, and the Spirit what is contrary to the sinful nature. They are in conflict with each other, so that you do not do what you want. But if you are led by the Spirit, you are not under law.

GALATIANS 5:14–18 ❧

❧ Your Turn

- In your experience, how does the work of the Holy Spirit enable us to transcend self-centeredness?
- Give an example of a time when you set aside selfish concerns to be more loving toward your partner? Looking back, can you see any fruit that your choice produced in your marriage?

REAL-LIFE SOUL MATES

When we got married thirty years ago, we were convinced that God had brought us together and we determined that whatever circumstances we might face, we would remain committed to each other and committed to making our marriage work.

We have not always given our marriage the attention it deserves. Too often we have coasted along, caught up in other things, not thinking about our relationship. But our intimacy as a couple has grown because we still believe in *commitment*.

We also believe in *faithfulness*. After all these years we feel a tremendous sense of peace and satisfaction to know that in a world filled with temptations (we've faced them) there are no "skeleton stories hidden in a closet." We have remained sexually and relationally faithful to each other. That builds intimacy as soul mates.

We pray together whenever we have crises, are making significant decisions, or reach difficult times in life. Unlike many couples, however, we have not prayed together consistently on a day-to-day basis (except before meals) and neither do we have a good track record with family devotions. But we do place a high value on *worship* as a couple. It is difficult sometimes to find a church with well-planned worship experiences that focus on Christ, but when we are able to praise God together with other believers in the body of Christ, we grow closer as soul mates.

For us, commitment, faithfulness, and worship have helped us to cultivate spiritual intimacy as a couple.

GARY AND JULIE COLLINS

- In what concrete ways is your life more "whole" now that you are married?
- When is the "individual survival mode" most likely to dominate your relationship? Give specific examples.
- Discuss in specific terms how you can work together to turn the balance of your marriage into a "we"-centered relationship.

❧ Soul to Soul

To deepen your spiritual intimacy this next week, make note of:

- What you gained from this session together.
- A pressure point in your partner's upcoming week you will pray about.
- A concrete kindness you can offer your partner this week.

❧ Prayer

Heavenly Father, it is your Spirit dwelling in our marriage that enables us to transcend our self-concern and more effectively love one another. Reveal to us the power of this principle to produce a fruitful, thriving, and enjoyable marriage. Strengthen us by your grace to be a partner characterized by all the fruit of your Spirit. Amen.

WHAT A DIFFERENCE A TEMPERAMENT MAKES!

After the great writer F. Scott Fitzgerald died, the executor of his estate found his notes on a play which was never written. The plot involved five members of one family who lived apart, but would inherit a stately mansion if they could agree to only one condition—to live in the house together.

Marriage is a little like that unfinished play. People who have been living apart are suddenly offered life's most compelling rewards if they can only learn how to live together.

The catch, of course, is that living together is not always easy. It requires maturity. Some have suggested that two strangers could be married to each other off the street and make a pretty good marriage together if only they were mature enough to work their way through the inevitable differences.

How do you and your partner handle differences? If you are like most couples you probably try one of two things: You either sweep your differences under the rug by ignoring them altogether, or you try to make your partner become like yourself. Unfortunately, both strategies are doomed to frustration. For one thing, it is only a matter of time before repressed differences reemerge, and second, we miss out on a tremendous gift of marriage when we do not enjoy our partner's uniqueness. That's right, enjoy the differences!

In Psalm 139:14 we read, "I praise you because I am fearfully and wonderfully made; your works are wonderful, I know that full well." Every person is unique. God never intended couples to approach life as if they were twins separated at birth. He made us with unique strengths and weaknesses. He gave each of us special gifts.

The New Testament uses the image of a human body to illustrate the church (see 1 Cor. 12:12). A body composed of many members with many gifts can accomplish far more than a one-celled organism. The same principle applies to marriage. The differences in temperament that allow your partner to deal with situations that would drive you crazy is something to be thankful for. Sure, some of his or her traits make living together tough at times, but appreciating the positive side of your differences will make your marriage more balanced and complete. And like the family in Fitzgerald's unfinished play, you will inherit the riches only soul mates enjoy.

FROM GOD'S WORD

If you have any encouragement from being united with Christ, if any comfort from his love, if any fellowship with the Spirit, if any tenderness and compassion, then make my joy complete by being like-minded, having the same love, being one in spirit and purpose. Do nothing out of selfish ambition or vain conceit, but in humility consider others better than yourselves. Each of you should look not only to your own interests, but also to the interests of others.

PHILIPPIANS 2:1–4 ❧

❧ Your Turn

- How do you and your partner handle differences? How could you improve the way you do this?
- Give an example of a time when your partner allowed the gift of your uniqueness to be evident in your marriage— a time when your differences were appreciated.

REAL-LIFE SOUL MATES

Fred and I spent the first fifteen years of our marriage trying to change each other. If only he would loosen up, laugh occasionally, and have fun, I could be happy. If only I would get serious, be on time, and check off the charts he had so carefully made, there might be some hope. We didn't understand each other, and even though we never yelled at one another, we were miserable inside. We knew how to do the right things, belong to the right clubs, live on the right side of town, and raise the right kind of children. But our right plans turned wrong when we produced two sons, one after another, who were born with a fatal brain defect.

Suddenly we faced a reality we had never anticipated. Keeping quiet about our differences and pretending to be happy didn't work anymore. At that point, fifteen years into a businesslike marriage, two things happened. First, we both committed our lives to the Lord Jesus in a personal and meaningful way; and second, we started a study of the four basic temperaments. I found out that I was the Popular Sanguine who wanted to have fun and Fred was the Perfect Melancholy who was depressed when all of life didn't add up in perfect columns. We both were also part the Powerful Choleric who wants to be in charge. I wanted to be in control and enjoy life. Fred wanted to be in charge and make everything and everybody perfect. What a blessing it was to find that we were born with different personalities and that different wasn't wrong. As soon as we accepted each other as we were, we invited couples into our home and began to teach them what we'd learned. We saw marriages changed right there in our living room. Soon we were asked to share in our church, and that was the beginning of a ministry that has spread around the world and spawned over twenty books on getting along with people who are nothing like us.

FRED AND FLORENCE LITTAUER

- How do you see the diversity of the body of Christ reflected in your marriage? In other words, how do your gifts differ from and complement one another?
- Discuss the tendency married people have to either change their partner or sweep differences under the rug. Where do you each fall on this continuum?
- What specific traits do each of you bring that create balance and completion in your marriage?

Soul to Soul

To deepen your spiritual intimacy this next week, make note of:
- What you gained from this session together.
- A pressure point in your partner's upcoming week you will pray about.
- A concrete kindness you can offer your partner this week.

Prayer

God of creation, teach us how to deal with the inevitable differences which are a part of marriage. Allow us to be grateful for these differences even when they first appear to be the source of our frustration. For our individual characteristics bring fullness to our marriage. So grant us the courage to acknowledge and to value our differences. Amen.

SESSION TEN:

IF YOU BUGGED YOURSELF, WHAT WOULD YOU HEAR?

Some scientists in Great Britain have come up with the idea that every word that has ever been spoken is still floating around out there somewhere in space. All we need, they say, is one more scientific breakthrough and we can bring in any conversation that has ever occurred. We can hear Lincoln give his Gettysburg Address, or Caesar deliver his orations in the halls of the senate in Rome. We could even hear the words of our Lord as he gave the Sermon on the Mount.

But think of the personal implications. What if our conversations could be replayed at will? What if your partner could say, "Let's listen to what you said last Tuesday about that topic"?

Have you ever listened to yourself on tape? As counselors in training, each of us had to record our counseling sessions and play them back with our supervisors. It's an educational but nerve-wracking experience. The supervisor plays the tape for a few minutes, then hits the pause button: "There, did you notice what you just said?"

Thank goodness no one has played back what we say to each other in our own homes. But researchers at Duke University have recorded conversations in other homes. For six weeks they surreptitiously taped family conversations over mealtimes. After tabulating the results, they discovered that most conversations can be categorized in one of five ways: (1) non-conversations, (2) critical-of-family conversations, (3) critical-of-others conversations, (4) materialistic conversations, and (5) discussions of issues and ideas.

If you bugged yourself, if you recorded the conversations between you and your partner, what would you hear? What category of conversation would top your list?

The prophet Isaiah didn't have the technical equipment for recording his conversations in ancient Jerusalem, but when he was only twenty-six years of age he took a personal inventory of his talk. And what he found didn't please him: "I am ruined! For I am a man of unclean lips, and I live among a people of unclean lips, and my eyes have seen the King, the LORD Almighty" (6:5).

Isaiah recognized negativism in himself. And, like you and me, he could have easily justified it. He was at a low point in his life: Everything had fallen to pieces with the death of the king and the failure of the regime which followed. Isaiah had plenty of personal disappointments to cope with. He could have fortified his negative attitude with his friends; they certainly would have fanned the flame of a critical conversation. But Isaiah chose a different route. And God met his need with a live coal "which he had taken with tongs from the altar. With it he touched my mouth and said, 'See, this has touched your lips; your guilt is taken away and your sin atoned for'" (6:7).

The things you choose to talk about will determine the tone of your marriage—whether it is upbeat or colored by negativism. So ask yourself, what would you hear if your conversations were recorded?

FROM GOD'S WORD

When we put bits into the mouths of horses to make them obey us, we can turn the whole animal. Or take ships as an example. Although they are so large and are driven by strong winds, they are steered by a very small rudder wherever the pilot wants to go. Likewise the tongue is a small part of the body, but it makes great boasts. Consider what a great forest is set on fire by a small spark. The tongue also is a fire, a world of evil among the parts of the body. It corrupts the whole person, sets the whole course of his life on fire, and is itself set on fire by hell....

With the tongue we praise our Lord and Father, and with it we curse men, who have been made in God's likeness. Out of the same mouth come praise and cursing. My brothers, this should not be.

JAMES 3:3–6, 9–10 ❧

❧ Your Turn

- How is the topic of our conversations related to our spiritual journey?
- Give an example of a conversation topic that you and your partner sometimes focus on that is not healthy or productive.
- If you recorded a typical conversation between you and your partner over dinner what would you hear? What topics come up most often?
- What type of conversation would your hear most often in the family you grew up in (critical of family, critical of others, materialistic, or issues and ideas)?
- What practical things can you do as a couple to avoid negative conversations?

❧ Soul to Soul

To deepen your spiritual intimacy this next week, make note of:

- What you gained from this session together.
- A pressure point in your partner's upcoming week you will pray about.
- A concrete kindness you can offer your partner this week.

REAL-LIFE SOUL MATES

Spirituality is a lifestyle. It is not a compartment of life—it is life. We strive to live for Christ in every moment by maintaining a level of spiritual authenticity that honors Christ. Easy? No. Rewarding? Definitely! But believe us, it takes effort. And it takes a mentor or guide to help along the way.

Through his writings, Henri Nouwen has been one of those guides. We have been most affected by his philosophy of "Solitude, Community, Ministry." He helped us understand that, like Jesus, we need to spend time alone with God. From this flows a desire for relating to others in authentic community. Community, in turn, always leads to serving others in ministry. These three practices bring vitality and life to our marriage and our walk with God.

On a regular basis we give to one another the gift of solitude: intentional, extended periods of time alone with God. And we guard that time as if it were our life's savings. In our house the cry, "Leave me alone!" is often answered, "OK." Solitude helps us escape the world but, more importantly, it helps us draw near to the Father who calls us his beloved. I know it sounds absurd to say, "We get closer by getting alone." But that is exactly what happens. So once a month one of us takes about two days to be alone with God.

BILL AND GAIL DONAHUE

❧ Prayer

Heavenly Father, thank you for the gift of communication. Help us to use it well. Keep us from allowing negativism to poison our conversations. Teach us to communicate wisely, conveying hope and encouragement to each other daily. Amen.

Session Eleven:
Sloppy Agape

In the early days of aviation, pilots often used a phrase which described the nature of their work: "Flying by the seat of your pants." Before sophisticated instruments were as widely available on planes as they are today, the only guide for air navigation in inclement weather was pure physical sensation. If the pilot felt pressure from the seat of the aircraft, it probably meant he was ascending, much the same as the feeling you get in a rising elevator. Conversely, if there was a sensation of weightlessness, it most likely meant the plane was on the descent. This means flying, of course, was not reliable. In fact it was flat-out dangerous. Men met their deaths because their feelings played tricks on their judgment.

Feelings can be just as deadly when they are used to navigate your way through a marriage. Jan, married only a couple of years to Mike, came to us because she could never seem to please him. "I'm not blaming Mike," Jan confided, "I just wish I could be a better wife. I do a lot for him, but it never seems to be enough." Jan took all the responsibility for Mike's happiness. And if he was not perfectly content—it was her fault!

Jan's marital happiness was at the mercy of her feelings. What's wrong with that? Well, when we use feelings to steer our marriage we end up doing loving things rather than being a loving person. We end up falling into a trap we call "sloppy agape."

This kind of love can look like the ultimate in selflessness, but it continually misses the mark. A classic biblical example of sloppy agape is found in Jesus' friend Martha. They first met when

Martha opened her home to Jesus and his disciples. Martha scurried about making preparations to serve the men, while her sister, Mary, simply sat and conversed with Jesus. Finally, Martha complained, "'Lord, don't you care that my sister has left me to do the work by myself? Tell her to help me!'

"'Martha, Martha,' the Lord answered. 'You are worried and upset about many things, but only one thing is needed. Mary has chosen what is better, and it will not be taken away from her'" (Luke 10:40–42).

Martha was more concerned with doing loving things in the kitchen than being a loving person in her relationship with Jesus. She was attending to everyone else's needs, but she did not recognize her own need to sit at the feet of Jesus. Only later, when her faith in Jesus had grown, was she able to put aside her own worries and trust him even in the worst of circumstances—when her beloved brother, Lazarus, had died.

Don't get caught in the sloppy agape trap. If you focus too much on your feelings you will end up meeting needs your partner doesn't really have. Scurrying around and desperately trying to please your partner will only lead to disappointment on both sides. So if you rely too much on your feelings, remember to focus not just on doing loving things but on being a loving person.

FROM GOD'S WORD

If I speak in the tongues of men and of angels, but have not love, I am only a resounding gong or a clanging cymbal. If I have the gift of prophecy and can fathom all mysteries and all knowledge, and if I have a faith that can move mountains, but have not love, I am nothing. If I give all I possess to the poor and surrender my body to the flames, but have not love, I gain nothing.

1 CORINTHIANS 13:1–3

REAL-LIFE SOUL MATES

When I asked Maggie how we had developed spiritual intimacy through our twenty-three years of marriage, her first response was to laugh. That worried me a bit.

We could both recall those early days of marriage when we would take time after the evening meal to read together through four chapters of the Bible. And then, as we reminisced, she reminded me that I often ended those times with my head slumped over my plate, sound asleep as she read the last two chapters. I recall now that we decided to change our approach after a scary incident one night when I almost drowned in the gravy.

Then we both thought of those times when we pray together in bed—sharing our thoughts, frustrations, and hopes at the end of a busy day. While this is not a nightly habit, those times are precious indeed. Unfortunately, the problem again is drowsiness winning out over fervency.

Maggie explained our developing spiritual intimacy this way: "You have given me this wonderful, complete freedom to seek God and nurture a deeper relationship with him."

We have always thought of our marriage as a triangular relationship. We are at the two lower angles and God is at the top. The closer we grow to Christ, the more diminished is the distance between us. As we become one with Christ, so do we become one with each other.

I spend time with God early each morning before the house wakes up and the music starts. Maggie enjoys a leisurely devotional time after everyone has left for school and work. Neither of us insists that the other be involved in our devotional habits. But we freely share what we are learning in our individual pursuit of God.

I would say that our spiritual intimacy is not shaped by a shared mutual devotional pattern as a couple, but rather it is shaped by a shared mutual pursuit of intimacy with Christ.

DUFFY AND MAGGIE ROBBINS

❧ Your Turn

- How have you allowed feelings to navigate your way through marriage? Be specific.
- Give an example of a time when you met a need of your partner's out of a compulsion to please or simply to feel like a loving person. Did it backfire?
- Discuss how you can support one another in activities that meet your deepest spiritual needs.
- How can you distinguish between your partner's feelings and his or her genuine needs? Discuss what signs to look for in each other.
- What practical things can you do as a couple to encourage a focus on being loving persons rather than doing loving things?

❧ Soul to Soul

To deepen your spiritual intimacy this next week, make note of:

- What you gained from this session together.
- A pressure point in your partner's upcoming week you will pray about.
- A concrete kindness you can offer your partner this week.

❧ Prayer

Lord of life, help us to love from a foundation of peace rather than frenzy. Quiet our souls in your presence so that we may seek to be loving persons rather than striving to do that which only appears loving. Lift us from the tyranny of sloppy agape and help us to love with genuine hearts. Amen.

Session Twelve:

It's My Marriage and I'll Cry If I Want To

"Don't cry!"

"It's okay to cry," Leslie whimpered.

We were having lunch at a favorite restaurant, talking about I don't know what when out of nowhere, or so it seemed, Leslie's eyes flooded with tears. Only moments before they were sparkling.

"I know it's okay to cry," I confessed, "but can't you wait until we get in the car?"

My simple request only exacerbated the emotion I was trying to stifle. Leslie dabbed her eyes with a napkin, trying to retain her mascara, but the floodgates soon opened and the tears flowed like a stream.

I can't tell you how many times we have lived through similar scenes and neither of us could tell you what the issues were, but we can assure you that tears are a part of every marriage relationship. And it's a good thing. Research on crying has shown that tears contain chemicals related to stress. When people cry they are actually washing away the harmful effects of stress. William Fry, in his book *Crying: The Mystery of Tears*, suggests that women, whom society allows to cry more openly and frequently, are able to excrete their "stress waste" more readily than men, who are conditioned to block this natural cleansing system.

Whatever the scientists have discovered about crying, God understood in the beginning. Did you know that God keeps a record of your tears? The psalmist says they are listed on a scroll (see Ps. 56:8). God values our tears. Consider who God chose to be his spokesperson at the most critical time in Israel's history— Jeremiah, "the weeping prophet"! Jeremiah didn't always have the words to describe his feelings, but his tears often served as his message. He was not ashamed to bury his head in his hands and sob aloud. He was not ashamed to cry.

How about you? When your words fail, can you let the tears flow? Can you identify with the woman in the opening chapter of Lamentations: "Bitterly she weeps at night, tears upon her cheeks" (1:2)? Can you identify with the prophet who said, "Streams of tears flow from my eyes because my people are destroyed. My eyes will flow unceasingly, without relief, until the LORD looks down from heaven and sees" (Lam. 3:48–51)? How about with Jesus as he wept at the death of his friend Lazarus (John 11:35)?

Let me be honest. I'm not totally comfortable with tears. When Leslie cries I still cringe. But I have learned that tears, hers and mine, are essential to a growing marriage. And I have learned to value the tears of my wife—just as God does.

Part of becoming soul mates is learning that there is no shame in tears. Sure, crying in the middle of a restaurant is nobody's idea of a good time, but if onlookers don't understand the tenderness of tears between a married couple, that's their problem!

FROM GOD'S WORD

And he who sits on the throne will spread his tent over them. Never again will they hunger; never again will they thirst. The sun will not beat upon them, nor any scorching heat. For the Lamb at the center of the throne will be their shepherd; he will lead them to springs of living water. And God will wipe away every tear from their eyes.

REVELATION 7:15–17 ❧

REAL-LIFE SOUL MATES

When Nancy and I got married, we were both a little disappointed in our spiritual connection with each other. After all, both of us would have told you that one of the most attractive things we found in each other was our sincere and deeply cultivated relationship with Jesus Christ. We had high hopes and expectations. And for several years our inability to have a "family altar" or "quiet time" together was a real source of pain.

I'm not sure just when, but somewhere along the line, God gave us both the grace to comprehend and accept that we are very different from each other when it comes to personality and spirituality styles. So we released each other to private prayer.

Remarkably, about the same time, I found myself feeling lonely and empty. One day, I all but forced Nancy to take a mid-day ride out to a marina on Puget Sound near our house. It was there that I broke out in tears (not a frequent occurrence) and said, "Honey, I love you and I really, really need you."

I think this experience of "needing" led us to begin valuing intentional time together to play, relax, and talk. This "marriage fellowship" has become a great spiritual discipline, not unlike the fellowship which nurtured the earliest Christians (Acts 2:38–47). Our regular Monday night date from 5:30 P.M. until bedtime has become a spawning ground of spiritual strength for each of us. In addition, we have expanded this "spirituality through covenant fellowship" idea beyond the two of us to a ten-person couple's group with whom we spend from 7:00 to 10:00 P.M. every other Friday.

Fellowship is our key connecting point as we release each other to be people who have "devoted themselves to the Apostle's teaching, to fellowship, the breaking of bread and prayer."

RANDY AND NANCY ROWLAND

❧ Your Turn

- How have tears played a part in your marriage? How would each of you rate on a "tearfulness scale"?
- Give an example of a time you personally cried with your spouse. How comfortable was that experience for you?
- How does Christ's response to the death of Lazarus impact you? What does it tell you about expressing your feelings through tears?
- Discuss how your spiritual well-being may be linked to your emotional well-being in marriage?
- How can each of you more effectively take into account the emotional well-being of your partner? How can you give him or her the freedom to express even sad emotions?

❧ Soul to Soul

To deepen your spiritual intimacy this next week, make note of:

- What you gained from this session together.
- A pressure point in your partner's upcoming week you will pray about.
- A concrete kindness you can offer your partner this week.

❧ Prayer

God of compassion, you who have known true joy and experienced true sorrow, help us to understand our emotions deeply. Enable us to draw on the gift of tears as a source of strength for our marriage. Let us learn, even this week, to be comfortable with tears in our marriage. Amen.

Session Thirteen:
Rapunzel's Love Lesson

The fairy tale "Rapunzel" is the story of a beautiful young girl imprisoned in a tower with an old witch who insistently tells her she is ugly. One day when Rapunzel gazes from the window in her tower, she sees her Prince Charming standing below. He is enchanted by her beauty and tells her to let her long, golden tresses down from the window. The prince then braids her hair into a ladder and climbs up to rescue her.

The implicit message of this fairy tale is simple but profound. Rapunzel's prison is really not the tower but her fear that she is ugly and unlovable. The mirroring eyes of her prince, however, tell her that she is loved, and thus she is set free from the tyranny of her own imagined worthlessness.

In a sense, we are all, like Rapunzel, enslaved by the fear of rejection, yearning to be valued by a prince or princess. But in our counseling office we have seen enough couples to know that some spouses are especially troubled by the fear of being unlovable. They are afraid that they are not loved because they feel unlovable. Susan, married just under a year, came to us with her husband, Don, because she repeatedly questioned her worth. "Sometimes I just don't know how Don can love me," she would say. "I feel so guilty; like I don't deserve to have such a good husband."

Jonah would have understood Susan's feelings of inadequacy. When God called Jonah to preach to the city of Nineveh, Jonah ran away. And when a storm threatened to capsize the boat he was on, Jonah knew immediately whose fault the storm was. "Throw me into the sea," he said, "and it will become calm" (1:12). Only when he was trapped in the belly of the great fish did Jonah stop running and face up to God.

Sometimes love is a difficult gift to grasp. The grace of being loved and accepted unconditionally is incomprehensible. And though our partner will certainly fall short of this kind of perfect love, we must still come to accept the gracious gift of God's eternal love: "For God so loved the world that he gave his one and only Son, that whoever believes in him shall not perish but have eternal life" (John 3:16).

Like Rapunzel or like Susan, some of us fear that we are not lovable, that even a prince or princess cannot change that. And some of us, like Jonah, cannot fathom why God would choose us to love. That is why John reminds us: "As the Father has loved me, so have I loved you. Now remain in my love" (John 15:9).

FROM GOD'S WORD

Therefore, there is now no condemnation for those who are in Christ Jesus, because through Christ Jesus the law of the Spirit of life set me free from the law of sin and death. For what the law was powerless to do in that it was weakened by the sinful nature, God did by sending his own Son in the likeness of sinful man to be a sin offering. And so he condemned sin in sinful man, in order that the righteous requirements of the law might be fully met in us, who do not live according to the sinful nature but according to the Spirit.

ROMANS 8:1–4

❧ Your Turn

- Why do you think it is difficult to accept God's gracious unconditional love?
- Give an example of how your personal significance was recently affirmed by your partner.

REAL-LIFE SOUL MATES

Over the years, my wife, Cindy, and I have taken specific passages that we have studied in God's Word and used them as a "personalized prayer guide" for each other. For example, take Psalm 15. That's a wonderful psalm where David lists ten traits that should be reflected in each Christian's life, then caps them off with a promise, "He who does these things will never be shaken."

With all the ups and downs of living in a stressful world, an "unshakable life" is certainly something we both want to have! So we've taken the ten traits listed there and specifically prayed that they will be daily reflected in our loved one's life.

For example, "He who walks with integrity, works righteousness and speaks truth in his heart," becomes a personalized prayer for my wife: "Lord, may you keep Cindy walking in integrity; may she choose to do the right thing today, even in those times when it's difficult; and may your Word so fill her heart that her words to herself and to others echo your truth." Or, to apply another verse of Psalm 15 ("He swears to his own hurt and does not change"), she would pray for me, "Lord, may John be a man who always keeps his promises. Even if it's costly. Lord, may he always put commitment ahead of convenience."

Studying a passage together, then praying that God's truth will deeply reside in each other's life is a great way to build spiritual bonds!

JOHN AND CINDY TRENT

- Have you been trapped in the prison of fear of rejection?
- What is one thing your partner can do to affirm your worth and value?
- Discuss ways you can work as a couple to strengthen your awareness of God's love and grace this week.

❧ Soul to Soul

To deepen your spiritual intimacy this next week, make note of:

- What you gained from this session together.
- A pressure point in your partner's upcoming week you will pray about.
- A concrete kindness you can offer your partner this week.

❧ Prayer

Gracious God, grant us this week the power to live in full knowledge of your unconditional love. And help us to give the same unconditional love to each other. At times it is tough, so we ask you to keep us motivated. Thank you for your love to us. Amen.

SESSION FOURTEEN:
LISTENING
WITH THE THIRD EAR

"The road to the heart," wrote Voltaire, "is the ear." So true. Carefully listening to your partner is the quickest path to intimacy. The problem is that most of us confuse hearing with listening. There is a simple skill, however, that can immediately help most couples improve their ability to really listen. It is called reflection.

Like a mirror reflecting an image, good listeners reflect the emotions of the people they are with. Here are some examples:

> Husband: I don't care what my boss says, I'm not giving up those vacation days.
> Wife: You sound pretty resolved.

> Wife: I can't believe they canceled the party. I was so excited for this thing.
> Husband: You sound really disappointed.

Listening to what your partner is feeling is far more important than hearing what they are saying. Theodore Reik calls it listening with "the third ear." It allows you to tap into the emotional message that underlies nearly every verbal message. And when you can do this for each other, you immediately strengthen your bond as soul mates.

By the way, reflective listening is the best way we know of to defuse a potential conflict. If your partner starts hurling "you" statements such as "You are always late," try not to become defensive by saying, "I am not." Instead, reflect the emotional message by saying, "I know it upsets you when I'm late. It's got to be exasperating." The point is to listen for the message underlying the actual words. "You are always late" means "I'm upset."

Jesus understood this. When he encountered the emotionally disturbed demonic man who lived among the tombs in Gadara, the man was shouting at Jesus: "What do you want with us, Son of God? Have you come here to torture us?" (Matt. 8:29). Jesus could have turned and walked away. He certainly didn't deserve to be talked to like that. Jesus would have been justified in leaving the poor man to his own devices. But instead, Jesus listened with the third ear. He not only heard the words that the man shouted, but he listened for the message of the emotions behind the words. Jesus understood that the man's outburst was really a cry for help.

Since most people talk at the rate of 120 words per minute, and since most spoken material can be comprehended equally well at rates up to 250 words per minute, plenty of extra time is available for mental activity during a typical conversation. So instead of using that time to think of what you want to say next, use it to tap into the emotions of your partner. Use it to listen with the third ear.

FROM GOD'S WORD

Do not let any unwholesome talk come out of your mouths, but only what is helpful for building others up according to their needs, that it may benefit those who listen.

EPHESIANS 4:29 ✿

REAL-LIFE SOUL MATES

We try to keep our marriage fresh in the following ways.

We **talk**. Shortly after we were first married, we both woke up at about 2:00 A.M. wide awake. That night, we watched an old film on TV. Although the movie wasn't bad, we decided that we could spend our times in a more profitable venture—talking. And we have. About once a month, we have those unplanned 2:00 A.M. to 4:00 A.M. discussions. And we work hard at talking at more normal times as well. At least four times a day we talk on the phone and checkin briefly. We think we're getting better at this with age. The more we talk, the better we are at it.

We **think**. One way we have maintained a closeness is that we think about common issues. When one of us is struggling with an issue related to work, we think about it together. When we're wrestling with an issue about home or kids or relationships, we think together. We value each other's minds. We don't separate roles or responsibilities in such a way that we are out of touch with one another. We want to be partners in all we do, and this thinking process not only makes us more effective, it also makes us better friends.

We **try**. Oh, how we try. We try to pray together and fail more than we succeed. We try to get date nights each week only to find a date night taken by a kid's ball game. We try to read the Bible together as a family and it's hit-and-miss. We try to keep in touch with friends because we know that a network of those who care helps. When depression is only an inch away, we try to have "picnics in the storms" instead of giving in to discouragement. On most days, we give it our best efforts. We have tried so much that we understand that perfection will only occur in heaven. So we don't give up and that process makes our marriage stronger.

DENNY AND MARILYN RYDBERG

❧ Your Turn

- How do each of you practice the art of reflective listening? What do you consciously do to make it work?
- Give an example of how you personally have practiced the art of listening with your partner. What made it difficult or easy?
- Does reflective listening come more easily to one of you than it does to the other? Why or why not?
- How does listening relate to your spiritual journey?
- What is one way you can each practice reflective listening to strengthen the bonds of your marriage this week?

❧ Soul to Soul

To deepen your spiritual intimacy this next week, make note of:

- What you gained from this session together.
- A pressure point in your partner's upcoming week you will pray about.
- A concrete kindness you can offer your partner this week.

❧ Prayer

Gracious God, you who listen to the messages often buried beneath the words in our prayers, create in us the capacity to listen to each other as you listen to us. Through the inspiration of your Holy Spirit, enlighten, instruct, and guide us in the art of listening this week. Amen.

❧

IS PRAYER YOUR STEERING WHEEL OR YOUR SPARE TIRE?

Praying together is not easy for us. Oh, we pray as a couple before meals, and we pray together when there is a special need or crisis, but we aren't the kind of couple who kneels beside our bed each night. We might be better persons if we did, but we don't. I suppose we could blame our busy and fickle schedules, but the truth is we just haven't made the effort to build a consistent shared prayer time into our lives.

We admire couples who do and we covet the rewards they surely reap. For as Jesus has said, "If two of you on earth agree about anything you ask for, it will be done for you by my Father in heaven. For where two or three come together in my name, there am I with them" (Matt. 18:19–20).

Still, one thing we do every day is pray for each other. Whether together or in separate cities, we remember each other in our daily prayers. We made that commitment on our wedding day and Leslie had the reference of Philippians 1:3–11 engraved inside my wedding band. It's a prayer that says, "I thank my God every time I remember you.... I always pray with joy because of your partnership in the gospel from the first day until now."

Sometimes one of us will say to the other, "I'll be praying for you today," but most of the time there is just a quiet assurance that our partner is lifting us up with prayers.

"Prayer—secret, fervent, believing prayer—lies at the root of all personal godliness," wrote William Carey. Prayer transports us into the deepest levels of the human spirit. It is in prayer that we begin to think God's thoughts and desire the things he desires (see Rom. 8:26–27). And we believe that praying for each other is critically important to guiding soul mates. Corrie ten Boom asks a poignant question about prayer that every couple should answer: "Is prayer your steering wheel or your spare tire?"

The great giants of the faith viewed prayer as the main source of direction in their lives. Martin Luther declared, "I have so much business I cannot get on without spending three hours daily in prayer." John Wesley said, "God does nothing but in answer to prayer," and he backed up his conviction by devoting two hours daily to praying. The words of Mark, "Very early in the morning, while it was still dark, Jesus got up, left the house and went off to a solitary place, where he prayed," stand as a commentary on the lifestyle of Jesus (1:35).

Fortunately, you don't have to be a "giant in the faith" to pray daily. In fact, you may just be learning to pray (even the disciples, in Luke 11:1, implored Jesus, "Lord teach us to pray"). But as long as you are spending time in prayer, you can be assured that God will make himself present in your life and in your marriage.

FROM GOD'S WORD

When you pray, do not be like the hypocrites, for they love to pray standing in the synagogues and on the street corners to be seen by men. I tell you the truth, they have received their reward in full. But when you pray, go into your room, close the door and pray to your Father,

who is unseen. Then your Father, who sees what is done in secret, will reward you. And when you pray, do not keep on babbling like pagans, for they think they will be heard because of their many words. Do not be like them, for your Father knows what you need before you ask him.
MATTHEW 6:5–8 ❧

❧ Your Turn

- Why do you think Jesus preached against hypocrites who love to pray in public? Why did he preach against "babbling" prayers?
- What were your experiences of prayer in your family growing up?
- Give an example of a time when you offered intercessory prayer for your partner. How did it impact your role in the situation at hand?
- Talk with your partner about the times you spend in personal prayer. Discuss how often you pray for each other.
- What can you do, in practical terms, to keep from treating prayer as a spare tire—only for emergencies?

❧ Soul to Soul

To deepen your spiritual intimacy this next week, make note of:

- What you gained from this session together.
- A pressure point in your partner's upcoming week you will pray about.
- A concrete kindness you can offer your partner this week.

REAL-LIFE SOUL MATES

Five o'clock this morning I was wide awake. Something troubling was on my mind.

Jill stirred slightly. "Are you awake?" I whispered.

"Oh yes," she replied, "About a couple of hours ago."

"Are you thinking about it?" I asked.

"Of course," she replied, "can't get it out of my mind."

"Do you want to talk about it?" I ventured.

"What is there new to say?" she responded.

"So let's pray about it," I suggested.

But what to pray? What could we say that we hadn't said before?

"You go first," I said.

"No, you," she countered, "Okay?"

Where to begin? My acrostic that I'd taught a hundred times—Praise, Repent, Ask, Yourself—didn't seem right.

Too stiff. Praying wouldn't come. I felt as cold as the Wisconsin February morning outside the window. So I just started to tell the Lord what was going on inside me. As I did so, Jill's hand searched for mine and held it tight. Her grip said, "That's what I think, that's how I feel. Go on, go on." The words began to form, the feelings began to flow, the petitions and longings became apparent. I stopped and she carried right on without a break. Adding to what I had said, remembering what I had omitted, repeating those words which framed her thoughts, and articulating my words with her own.

Two hearts beating as one. Two pray-ers, one Lord, one faith, one burden, one hope.

Praying together binds on earth two people whose hearts are bound to the One in heaven. It is one of marriage's deepest joys and greatest blessings.

STUART AND JILL BRISCOE

❧ Prayer

Gracious God, teach us to pray with meaning. Save us from the torrent of words which may be our cover-up for reality. Let us be authentic with our prayers and remind us this week to be grateful for every good quality we see in each other. Help us to surround our soul mate in prayer and sustain our marriage covenant through your grace. Amen.

SESSION SIXTEEN:
THE DEADLY EMOTION OF ANGER

It would be tough to find another emotion that has caused married couples more difficulty than anger. Why do we get angry at the person we love the most? Why do we allow ourselves to get angry when we know in advance that we will need to apologize? Why do we raise our voices when it does no good?

We have seen firsthand in our marriage counseling how different people use different means for dealing with their anger. Some try to deny it by calling it something else. They confuse anger with fatigue, nervousness, or being uptight. Others try to deal with their anger by suppressing it. They make every effort to keep it from showing (this usually leads to a phony, emotional, saccharine sweetness). Still others try to spiritualize their anger by talking about anger that is righteous and anger that is unrighteous (which usually means "my anger is righteous and yours is the other kind"). We have even seen some couples where one partner flaunts anger: "This is the way God made me. You know what I am like so you just might as well get used to it. It's in my genes."

Well, anger is not inherited. How we express our anger is learned and can be unlearned. Whether suppressed, spiritualized, or flaunted, anger will do its destructive deeds to even the best of marriages—unless we first of all understand what it is.

Anger begins as a physiological response to a real or imagined threat. The involuntary nervous system goes to work whenever the brain signals that injury is a possibility. First, sweat breaks out in the palms of our hands. Then the heart begins to pound twice as hard as usual. The throat gets dry. The pituitary gland pours adrenaline into the bloodstream, and suddenly the body is ready for battle.

Any attempt to spiritualize this involuntary response is futile. It is neither moral nor immoral. It is simply the body's response as God made us. But out of this response can come terrible behavior. This is why Paul wrote to the Ephesians, "In your anger do not sin: Do not let the sun go down while you are still angry" (4:26).

You see, it is not whether you get angry or not, but what you do with your anger once it kicks in. Paul encourages us to "be careful to do what is right … [and] live at peace with everyone"(Rom. 12:17–18). He warns us, "Do not take revenge" (Rom. 12:19).

FROM GOD'S WORD

Do not repay anyone evil for evil. Be careful to do what is right in the eyes of everybody. If it is possible, as far as it depends on you, live at peace with everyone. Do not take revenge, my friends, but leave room for God's wrath, for it is written: "It is mine to avenge; I will repay," says the Lord. On the contrary: "If your enemy is hungry, feed him; if he is thirsty, give him something to drink. In doing this, you will heap burning coals on his head." Do not be overcome by evil, but overcome evil with good.

ROMANS 12:17–21 ❧

❧ Your Turn

- What is the difference between feeling angry and committing a sin? Some believe they are the same thing. What about you?
- Give an example of a time when your partner's response enabled you to transform your anger into a positive outcome. What can both of you learn from that?

REAL-LIFE SOUL MATES

Dorothy and I were married in 1939. That's a long time ago!

I owe an immense debt of gratitude to Dorothy in my spiritual life and walk, because it was through her influence as college freshmen that I came to a personal relationship with Jesus Christ as Lord and Savior. As a result of this spiritual connection early on in our college careers, we began our love affair which has continued beyond a half century.

Early on we agreed that a rule of thumb for us in our marriage would be "no surprises." We have found that nothing replaces open communication channels for husbands and wives. Sometimes this hurts, but it is always necessary! Candor and openness by both parties—these are the key elements in a continual cultivation of spiritual intimacy.

It goes without saying that reading the Word together and praying together are vitally important. But beyond these is the vital necessity of keeping the communication lines open daily. As I travel—and have done so worldwide for a half century—I make sure, if at all possible, that I telephone Dorothy every night to let her know of my day and learn of her day's activities. This helps keep the spark of love alive— even after more than fifty-five years!

TED AND DOROTHY ENGSTROM

- Have you ever confused fatigue, nervousness, or being uptight with anger? How can you avoid this common error?
- What can you do, in practical terms, to resolve anger before it erupts? What can you do, for example, before discussing a typically hot issue?
- Since anger is inevitable, how can you and your partner work together to anticipate and deal with it constructively?

⁂ Soul to Soul

To deepen your spiritual intimacy this next week, make note of:

- What you gained from this session together.
- A pressure point in your partner's upcoming week you will pray about.
- A concrete kindness you can offer your partner this week.

⁂ Prayer

Our Father in heaven, you who are slow to anger and quick to show compassion, empower us to use our anger constructively. We accept anger as part of being human, but please save us from destructive anger or from the sin of using anger to manipulate each other. When we feel angry help us to call on you for guidance. Amen.

⁂

SESSION SEVENTEEN:
THE EXTRA MILE IN MARRIAGE

One of the most shocking statement Jesus ever made holds enough power to revolutionize your marriage.

He said:

If someone forces you to go one mile, go with him two miles.

Have you learned to apply the extra mile principle to your marriage? Every husband and every wife knows how to walk the first mile. After all, our relationships couldn't survive without it. The first mile is what we know we have to do. It is taking the trash out, preparing dinner, or balancing the checkbook because we said we would do it.

So what's the second mile? At the time Jesus made this statement, the Roman army had a pesky practice of forcing men and boys who were nearby to carry its soldier's packs. Being more civilized than other armies, the Romans limited the task to one mile. And every boy under Roman rule knew exactly how far that was. In fact, a boy often drove a stake into the ground precisely one mile from his house as a marker. This way, when a soldier required the task, the boy would walk exactly a mile down the road to the stake, set the pack on the other side and be done with it. That was all he was required and nobody expected more.

Jesus used this illustration to point out that we sometimes do the same thing in our relationships. We measure out exactly how much is expected and do just that, nothing more. Let's face it, with our hectic pace, most of us do just enough to squeak by even in the relationship that matters most. So, yes, we grumble and take the trash out or we whine and make the meal, but only because we have to. Jesus, however, says there is a better way—to do more than the minimum.

The extra mile turns the ordinary into the extraordinary, the expected into the unexpected. You walk the extra mile for your partner, for example, when you take the trash out with a smile or prepare a meal with a special touch. The extra mile turns responsibility into opportunity. When you are walking the extra mile in marriage your attitude shifts from "have to" to "want to." That's why the apostle Peter said, "Offer hospitality to one another without grumbling" (1 Peter 4:9).

Common courtesy is an example of the extra mile in some marriages. It sounds funny, but courtesy isn't so common after even a short period of marriage. We take "thank yous" and "you're welcomes" for granted. We forget to say "please" at the table. The apostle Paul understood the importance of this principle in our relationships. He urges us to be kind and loving toward one another (Gal. 5:22).

So practice the extra mile in your marriage. It is more powerful than dynamite. Try it.

FROM GOD'S WORD

And if someone wants to sue you and take your tunic, let him have your cloak as well. If someone forces you to go one mile, go with him two miles. Give to the one who asks you, and do not turn away from the one who wants to borrow from you.

MATTHEW 5:40–42

REAL-LIFE SOUL MATES

Spiritual intimacy really came to life for my wife and me when I committed my life to Christ on July 4, 1972. I immediately knew that I had a lot of catching up to do. But with my new spiritual commitment, my wife's spiritual growth also increased and our relationship improved immeasurably.

Four practices have been especially significant in our spiritual growth. First, we attended a Christian Marriage Encounter weekend and learned how to express our love for each other better. Second, we read the *One-Year Bible* together. Even though my travels took me out of town a great deal, I called her each evening at an appointed time and we discussed what the day's Scriptures had meant to each of us. Third, every day we each try to do something for the other that the other is completely capable of doing for him or herself. For instance, my wife has not opened her car door a half-dozen times since I became a Christian. Each time I walk around the car I'm reminded that here is the most important person on earth to me. Alternately, when I arise in the morning she will ask me if I'm ready for my tea or coffee and I'll say, "Yes, but I'll get it." Her response is, "No, let me do it." Fourth, we hug fifteen to thirty times each day. These are neither long nor sensual, but they communicate our love in a significant manner.

These steps are simple, but they have advanced our spiritual walk and developed our love for one another.

ZIG AND JEAN ZIGLAR

❧ Your Turn

- Why do you think Christ was so shocking in his definition of love? Do you believe it is obtainable?
- How have you struggled with the extra mile principle? Have weariness or business been obstacles for you? What else makes the extra mile in marriage difficult for you?
- What price do most couples pay for doing only the bare minimum, only what is expected in marriage?
- Give an example of a time when you benefited from the extraordinary love of your partner.
- How can you work together to practice the extra mile principle in your marriage? Give some examples of ways you might walk the extra mile for one another.

❧ Soul to Soul

To deepen your spiritual intimacy this next week, make note of:

- What you gained from this session together.
- A pressure point in your partner's upcoming week you will pray about.
- A concrete kindness you can offer your partner this week.

❧ Prayer

Gracious God, teach us to love each other as you love us. Teach us to walk the extra mile in patience, forgiveness, and kindness when we may be tempted this week to get by with the bare minimum. Give us the quality of gratitude that spills over to moments of courtesy and unexpected love in our marriage. In the name of Christ, amen.

❧

SESSION EIGHTEEN:
HELP FOR THE ROMANTICALLY IMPAIRED

It was our one-year anniversary—June 30, 1985. Whew! A whole year of being married. And now the celebration. Just how would we commemorate this important milestone? A romantic dinner and a walk under the stars? A rosy bouquet or a box of Godiva Chocolates? Nope. We packed a picnic lunch with tuna fish sandwiches and Diet Pepsi and drove from Pasadena up the coast to Santa Barbara, three or so hours away. It was Les's idea. *Okay*, I thought, *this could be fun*. We'll have time to talk as we drive and we can eat our lunch on the beach. But Les, now in graduate school, had a different idea. He was one week into a stressful summer school course, taking Greek! So he brought along a taped lecture to listen to on our drive and a pack of flash cards to study for his next exam.

So much for romance, at least on that day. I shouldn't paint an incorrect picture; Les can be very romantic. On my birthday this year, for example, he took me to the swankiest restaurant in town and had prearranged with the maître d' to have a gift delivered to our table with my favorite dessert.

Still, in our home, romance can be a hit-or-miss endeavor. Of course, I do my part. Like the time I planned a weekend getaway as a surprise for Les. That's when I learned he doesn't think surprises are very romantic! Or the time I thought he would enjoy going to a theater production instead of skiing with his friends. He didn't.

Well, if you don't already know, we haven't discovered *the* secret to romance in marriage. Maybe that makes us romantically impaired. But we have discovered that a big part of cultivating romance is learning to accept and respect each other's differences. Why? Because what is romantic to one person is not necessarily enjoyable to the other. For example, if Les has an unfinished task hanging over his head, I know to wait till he is done. Then he is fully present and ready to go out on the town. On the other hand, when I have a looming deadline hanging over my head, Les knows I love to be surprised with a diversion.

So Les is a little more practical, and I'm a little more frivolous. Does this affect our ability to cultivate romance? You bet. But what about you? What differences might impede your romantic endeavors? Can you accept and respect those differences? When Paul wrote to the Romans he said, "Accept one another, then, just as Christ accepted you" (15:7). I don't know if romance is what Paul had in mind with that advice, but it certainly applies.

FROM GOD'S WORD

Above all, love each other deeply, because love covers over a multitude of sins. Offer hospitality to one another without grumbling. Each one should use whatever gift he has received to serve others, faithfully administering God's grace in its various forms.

1 PETER 4:8–10 ❧

❧ Your Turn

- Scripture says that "love covers over a multitude of sins." What does this mean to you and how does it apply to marriage?
- Give an example of a time when you tried to be romantic with your partner and it didn't turn out that way. Are you able to laugh about it?

REAL-LIFE SOUL MATES

Last night the temperature plummeted close to zero degrees Fahrenheit. Since we normally heat the house with our woodstove, the bedroom was cold when we climbed into bed. Fortunately, that only made us more eager to snuggle closely together in each other's arms for our regular bedtime prayers under the covers.

For many years we have enjoyed starting and ending most days by praying together in each other's arms. We pray about the day's special worries and pressing problems, and often the prayer gets interrupted while we share a joy or sorrow we had forgotten to mention over dinner or dishes. Together we lift each other's biggest burdens to the Lord. And there's always time to ask God to watch over our children.

Devotional snuggling also helps us get over angry quarrels. You cannot hold onto your resentment if you honestly start to open your heart to the Heavenly Father.

Those few minutes of warmth and closeness with each other and with openness and petition to God have become regular moments of quiet joy and tenderness. And just a little more time for prayer is an unbeatable excuse to delay jumping out of bed on a sleepy morning.

We would be the first to confess that the warm feelings we experience in our devotional snuggling are not limited to the pleasure that flows from prayer. We are also certain that the God who inspired the Song of Songs does not mind at all. After all, both physical and spiritual intimacy were his idea.

RONALD AND ARBUTUS SIDER

- How is your partner's idea of romance different from yours? Discuss your idea of the perfectly romantic day or evening.
- In what specific ways do you appreciate your partner's "romance language"—even when it is different from your own?
- The romance that couples enjoy decades after their wedding is often the result of how they built romance into their early years together. What are you doing to make romance a natural part of your marriage?

❧ Soul to Soul

To deepen your spiritual intimacy this next week, make note of:
- What you gained from this session together.
- A pressure point in your partner's upcoming week you will pray about.
- A concrete kindness you can offer your partner this week.

❧ Prayer

Our Father, we thank you for creating in us the joy of romantic love. Grant us the ability to spark the heart of each other by responding to the need for tenderness. Help us receive the gifts of romantic love from our partner with joy. Amen.

Session Nineteen:
Our Longing for Belonging

Several weeks ago a number of couples from our church were gathered around a long restaurant table on a Sunday evening. We were in one of those peculiar seating arrangements where the wives were at one end of the table and the husbands at the other. When we began placing our orders with the server, the first person in a couple, for the sake of the bill, would say, "I belong to him," or "he belongs to me." No one around this table of fellowshiping couples was a loner. Everyone belonged to someone else.

It is wonderful to belong. Belongingness is an awareness of being wanted and accepted, of being cared for and enjoyed. It is the "we" feeling experienced when we know our partner appreciates us and wants to be with us. Belonging, however, doesn't begin in marriage. We begin the quest for belonging as soon as we enter the world. As infants and children we must be nurtured into a sense of belongingness with our family. In the turbulent teen years we try desperately to belong, to be with the "in" crowd. And certainly as young adults we long to belong.

But something wonderful happens in the quest for belongingness when we get married. By joining with another person for life, belongingness has an altogether new opportunity to flourish. There is a deep sense of belonging that comes with being soul mates.

A healthy marriage cannot survive without a sense of belonging. While marriage can survive great inconvenience, job loss, and physical illness, it can never survive rejection and aloneness. A married couple may have all the material things they can possibly need, but if they do not have a sense of belonging together they will starve emotionally. As Victor Hugo put it, "The supreme happiness of life is in the conviction that we are loved."

How are feelings of belongingness generated? By doing things together, by sharing common concerns, by trusting each other with responsibilities, by praying for each other, by laughing at things nobody else finds funny, by knowing what your partner is really thinking in a social setting, by sharing a meaningful insight, by doing nothing together. The list for cultivating belongingness could literally go on and on. Every couple has their own style of belonging.

But alas, our sense of belongingness, even in marriage, is only temporal compared to the belonging we enjoy as Christians. God has called us by name and we are his. "I tell you the truth, anyone who gives you a cup of water in my name because *you belong to Christ* will certainly not lose his reward" (Mark 9:41, italics added). We belong to God and he cares for us.

The ultimate source for generating belongingness in marriage is found in sharing a belonging to God.

FROM GOD'S WORD

Fear not, for I have redeemed you; I have summoned you by name; you are mine. When you pass through the waters, I will be with you; and when you pass through the rivers, they will not sweep over you. When you walk through the fire, you will not be burned; the flames will not set you ablaze. For I am the LORD, your God, the Holy One of Israel, your Savior.

ISAIAH 43:1–3 ❧

REAL-LIFE SOUL MATES

My wife and I have come to see life more and more as a war. Ultimately, our battle is with the forces of evil, but on a daily level war involves a struggle with time, money, priorities, health, and unplanned crisis. If we are to fight as allies, then we must grow in greater intimacy. To this growth we devote our time before dinner. This time is sacred and rarely crowded out by other activities. It is our R and R to return to fighting well.

This has required repeated instructions to our children not to interrupt us. It requires us to let the phone ring, to let guests wait for their hosts to return, and to offend countless others who see that as a selfish venture. In fact, it is a refueling time that allows us to engage with our world with a clearer loyalty to one another, a deepened passion for what is good, and a sense of rest that can come from no other place.

The time is seldom less than a half hour and occasionally may stretch for an hour. We usually begin by catching up on the events of the day. Soon, the events become the springboard for conversation about what was provoked in us that caused distress or delight. Often my wife will have read or thought about things that she recorded in her journal, and she will read to me. Other times I will want her to listen to something I have written. We find it crucial to read out loud together: It not only crystallizes our vague struggles, but it also records our progress together through life.

Our time is unstructured, but it is not uncommon for us to move from events to feelings, from a struggle to joy, or from reading to prayer. In conclusion and consummation we call on God to deepen our heart for him. We return to our family and world refreshed in our sense of being intimate allies.

DAN AND REBECCA ALLENDER

❧ Your Turn

- What do you think Christ means when he says he will make his home with us?
- Give an example of a time when you felt a keen sense of belonging with your partner. What made it so?
- When do you most often long to belong and in what ways?
- How was belongingness cultivated in your family as you were growing up?
- What is one thing you would like your partner to do to make you feel more like you "belong"? What is one thing you can do to create the same sense for your partner?

❧ Soul to Soul

To deepen your spiritual intimacy this next week, make note of:

- What you gained from this session together.
- A pressure point in your partner's upcoming week you will pray about.
- A concrete kindness you can offer your partner this week.

❧ Prayer

Dear Lord, we bow our heads and our hearts in respect of your presence within our lives and especially in our home. Increase our sense of belonging to you and to each other this week. The more you dwell within our marriage, the stronger our partnership and the deeper our conviction of our love will be. Amen.

❧

THE CHURCH:
A GREENHOUSE
FOR GROWING SOUL MATES

A friend of ours told us a funny story about two guys who were fishing fanatics. On a recent Sunday morning they arose at 4:00 A.M. and drove more than a hundred miles into the mountains expecting to catch trout in a favorite, secluded stream whose location they had kept secret for years. After hiking two miles in from the road their enthusiasm was dampened and the expedition aborted when they saw that rains farther upstream had produced silt, which muddied the waters and made fishing impractical. In their disgust one said to the other, "You might as well have stayed home and gone to church," to which his companion retorted with a straight face, "Oh, I can't go to church anyhow; my wife is sick."

How we choose to incorporate the church into our marriage is critically important in becoming soul mates. Research has shown that couples who attend church, even *once* a month, increase their chances of staying married. Studies have also shown that churchgoers feel better about their marriages than those who don't worship together. Attending church provides couples with a shared sense of values and purpose in life. It also provides couples with a caring community of support.

To cultivate spiritual intimacy in your marriage without incorporating the church is like trying to drive a car without a steering wheel. Billy Graham says that "churchgoers are like coals in a fire. When they cling together, they keep the flame aglow; when they separate, they die out." Charles Colson, in his book *The Body*, says, "There is no such thing as Christianity apart from the Church." The church is more than a group of people who come together. It is a group of people who are called together by the gospel of Christ's love and forgiveness. As Paul puts it, the church is called into "fellowship with [God's] Son" (1 Cor. 1:9).

Paul also recognized the idea of the church as being God's family when he said we are "members of God's household" (Eph. 2:19). When Jesus taught his disciples to pray he did not say, "my Father"; he said, "our Father" (Matt. 6:9). We cannot live the Christian life in isolation. Membership in the church is not some optional extra. We cannot be fully Christian without belonging to and participating in the church. The New Testament makes it clear that to be a Christian is to be "in Christ." This means being a member of the new society of which Christ is the living Head—the church.

From the beginning of our marriage, shared worship has been a systematic time of rest and renewal for our relationship. Dedicating a day of the week to attend church and worship with the body of Christ stabilizes our marriage and liberates us from the tyranny of productivity that fills our other days.

The church where we worship is a place of support and spiritual refueling. Singing hymns, learning from Scripture, worshiping God, and meeting with friends who share our spiritual quest is comforting and inspiring. Worshiping together buoys our relationship and makes the week ahead more meaningful.

FROM GOD'S WORD

Husbands, love your wives, just as Christ loved the church and gave himself up for her to make her holy, cleansing her by the washing with water through the word, and to present her to himself as a

REAL-LIFE SOUL MATES

The most significant factor in our growth together spiritually has been our intentional and intimate involvement with various small groups. Because we have very different temperaments, we discovered early in our marriage that we weren't very good at Bible study or even prayer on our own. We tried, but our best efforts seemed to turn often to a sense of failure. But we also realized that we didn't have to be alone in the process. The community of faith was and is God's great gift.

We were involved in small groups together right from the start. Sometimes they were intergenerational; sometimes focusing on couples; and sometimes involving a great diversity of people. But always the goal has been to grow in our relationship with Christ, with one another, and with Christ's work in the world.

In small groups we have heard one another share about what we were learning from Scripture and life. Our friends in the community of faith have encouraged, challenged, prayed, and wept with us. With our various small groups we have determined to glorify God in all that we do and to pray consistently for our marriage and family to be an encouragement to others. And through small groups our various spiritual gifts have been affirmed, and we have grown in our ministry side by side.

It is our conviction that marriage was never meant to be lived in isolation. Becoming true soul mates is a lifelong process. We are grateful for how far we have come, but we are also eager to go on learning and growing. And we are convinced that growth will happen best as we walk together with others.

STEPHEN AND SHAROL HAYNER

*radiant church, without stain or wrinkle or any other blemish, but
holy and blameless.*

EPHESIANS 5:25–27 ❧

❧ Your Turn

- Talk about the place worship holds for you as a couple.
  Rate its importance to you on a scale of one to ten.
- Give an example from your upbringing that illustrates the
  role worship has played in your life since you were a child.
- What are the goals you share as a couple for church
  involvement and how are you working to meet them?
- What is the highlight of the typical worship service for you?
  If it is the music, what is your favorite chorus or hymn?
- How can the two of you work to make worship as a
  couple more meaningful to both of you?

❧ Soul to Soul

To deepen your spiritual intimacy this next week, make note of:

- What you gained from this session together.
- A pressure point in your partner's upcoming week you will
  pray about.
- A concrete kindness you can offer your partner this week.

❧ Prayer

*Gracious God, grant us the strength, steadfastness, and
faithfulness to live in harmony with your body, the church,
in spite of its many human weaknesses. May our worship
bring us renewal as it brings you joy, and may our fellowship be a witness of your love and our unity. In Christ's holy
name we pray, amen.*

❧

Session Twenty-One:

Names Can Never Hurt Me—Or Can They?

Some years ago a team of psychologists did a study of a mill town in New England. Among other things, they were concerned with the criticism among the people who lived and worked so closely together. They found, first of all, that everyone in the community was guilty of criticizing everyone else. This was really no surprise. But they were really surprised to learn that all the community's members were absolutely scandalized whenever they heard that they themselves were the object of criticism. It was okay to criticize other people, but it was against the rules to be criticized.

Many sermons have been preached against criticism and its awful fruits. Many books have been written on the subject. But we are hard-pressed to find much of anything on how you are to respond in a marriage relationship when you inevitably become the object of your partner's criticism. It's an important issue. After all, you can do little to escape being criticized by the one who sees you up close, who knows how you live seven days a week. Being married is an act of opening yourself up to criticism. Sooner or later, whether he or she wants it to be critical or not, your partner will offhandedly critique something you do or even something you don't do.

In your contemplative moments you know that being criticized by your partner is part of "iron sharpening iron" (see Prov. 27:17), but that is little comfort when his or her iron seems to cut rather than polish. Being criticized by your spouse always hurts, probably because it contains a grain of truth. If your partner is like most people, he or she will pick some detail of your behavior and blow it all out of proportion. Even if you know it is simply an emotional exaggeration spurred on by a bad day at work, the truth buried in the criticism still stings.

No one was ever criticized more than Jesus. They called him a wine bibber, a glutton, one who enjoys the fellowship of sinners more than the company of good people. He was accused of being a Samaritan, which was the same as being a traitor. Few have suffered more hostile scrutiny and unfair critique than Christ. The question is: How did he respond?

Jesus could have lashed out verbally against his accusers. He could have called down angels from heaven to take care of his critics. In one instance his disciples encouraged him to burn up the village where he was not welcome (Luke 9:51–55). But Jesus never struck back. What did he do? He forgave his critics. And ultimately, his response to criticism came on the cross when he prayed, "Father, forgive them, for they do not know what they are doing" (Luke 23:34).

Christ's forgiveness is surely a sign of his divinity. The human response is not to forgive those who attack us, even when it is our spouse. We impulsively strike back with even louder accusations. But—and this is important—Christ can empower you with the same capacity to forgive. Scripture tells us to "bear with each other and forgive whatever grievances you may have against one another. Forgive as the Lord forgave you" (Col. 3:13).

FROM GOD'S WORD

In love he predestined us to be adopted as his sons through Jesus Christ, in accordance with his pleasure and will—to the praise of his glorious grace, which he has freely given us in the One he loves. In him we have redemption through his blood, the forgiveness of sins, in

REAL-LIFE SOUL MATES

Joyce and I were both in leadership positions in a parachurch organization when we got married. Our group's idealism was helpful in many ways, but it sometimes led to unrealistic expectations in our marriage. We were committed to pursuing the best in evangelism, Bible study, staff team relationships, and, of course, marriage.

At conference after conference, we heard speakers tell how they kept their marriages Christ-centered. The underlying message was, "If you do what we do, you'll have a great Christian marriage, too!" So we tried to pray like these couples prayed, study the Bible like these couples studied, and try everything anybody else ever said would benefit our marriage. After a few years of this, we were burned out!

In those early years, we made a commitment to pray together every night. And we did it—no matter what! Sometimes this was a rich experience, but gradually, it became a mere ritual. I remember telling Joyce, "Let's stop our commitment to pray every night. It doesn't mean as much to me anymore. From now on, let's pray more spontaneously." She agreed, and it was the beginning of fresh (if erratic) spiritual communication between us.

When we're talking about a difficult situation, it is natural to say, "Let's pray about it." We ask each other how we can pray specifically for one another, and we get updates of the answers to prayer. Certainly, we go through periods when we forget or get so busy we simply don't ask, but when we do, it is heartfelt and genuine.

Over the years, we learned—and continue to learn—that the spiritual techniques which "work" for other couples may or may not "work" for us. We have to find our own path, establish our own pattern, and cultivate our own communication with God and with each other.

PAT AND JOYCE SPRINGLE

*accordance with the riches of God's grace that he lavished on us with
all wisdom and understanding.*

EPHESIANS 1:4–8 ❧

❧ Your Turn

- Forgiveness is so fundamental to the message of Christ.
  What examples from Christ's life can you think of that
  illustrate this?
- Give an example of how you recently benefited from the
  ability of your partner to overlook a critical comment or
  behavior.
- When are you most likely to be critical of your partner?
- Have you talked about the difference between being criticized in public versus in private? What ground rules
  might help your relationship?
- How has your spouse's attentiveness and feedback contributed to your improvement? What works best for you
  in hearing critical information?

❧ Soul to Soul

To deepen your spiritual intimacy this next week, make note of:

- What you gained from this session together.
- A pressure point in your partner's upcoming week you will
  pray about.
- A concrete kindness you can offer your partner this week.

❧ Prayer

*Gracious God, empower us with the capacity to forgive
even when we have been under-valued or over-criticized
by our partner. We offer this prayer in sincerity and in the
name of Christ. Amen.*

❧

Session Twenty-Two:
Love Means Having to Eat Humble Pie

I did something dumb the other day. Leslie and I were driving in the bustling shopping section of downtown Seattle when I got an idea. "Hey, would you run in there and pick up a couple of those pens for me?" I asked Leslie. "I'll circle around the block and you can meet me on the corner." Leslie jumped out of the car and I began to circle.

Unfortunately, I was not very specific about which corner to meet her on. And then I discovered there were one-way streets I did not know about. The first thing I knew I had gone around many blocks and was trying desperately to get back on course. Finally I reached the corner where I thought Leslie would be. But she was on the other side of the street now, across two lanes of heavy traffic. I rolled down the window, honked the horn, and shouted, "Leslie, I'm over here!" She waved and made some motions I couldn't decipher. I waved back and ended up circling around four more blocks again to pick her up. You can guess what happened when she got into the car:

"What were you doing over there?" I snapped.

"What do you mean?" said Leslie. "You didn't tell me where to go, and I thought that was the corner you meant!"

We went around on this issue as much as I went around the city blocks. But once we both calmed down, I pulled the car over to the side and said those very difficult words that husbands have trouble saying: "I'm sorry."

I have a friend who has a saying I like. It always pops into my mind when I know I am wrong and should apologize. Here it is:

Humble pie is the only pastry that's never tasty.

Isn't that good? That goofy statement helps trigger my apology mechanism. After all, it's not easy to say "I'm sorry." Why? Because whenever we apologize we must first set aside our pride. Genuine sorrow is based on humility. There is no way around it. The writer of Proverbs understood this fact when he wrote: "When pride comes, then comes disgrace, but with humility comes wisdom" (11:2; see also 29:23).

I feel sorry for the person married to someone who never says, "I'm sorry." Without another piece of information about them, I can predict with confidence that their home is filled with conflict and quarrels. "Pride only breeds quarrels, but wisdom is found in those who take advice" (Prov. 13:10).

So remember, the next time you do something stupid, the next time you are in the wrong, 'fess up. Eat a little humble pie. It won't taste good, but it's the only sure way to say "I'm sorry."

FROM GOD'S WORD

Do nothing out of selfish ambition or vain conceit, but in humility consider others better than yourselves. Each of you should look not only to your own interests, but also to the interests of others. Your attitude should be the same as that of Christ Jesus.

PHILIPPIANS 2:3–5 ❧

❧ **Your Turn**

- The Bible underscores the importance of humility again and again. Why do you think humility is one of the marks of wisdom?

REAL-LIFE SOUL MATES

We are a team. We have collaborated in building a marriage, raising three children, and pursuing a variety of professional activities. We have also been a spiritual discovery team, each helping the other to grow in our faith. Our journey of discovery proceeds from the premise that whatever we plan or do is constrained by the fact that, for each of us, Jesus is Lord. We seek both in our personal lives and in our marriage to obey and serve him. And part of our commitment to each other is a commitment to nurture one another spiritually.

Honesty is fundamental to being a spiritual discovery team. It means that we don't use a fabricated piety as a weapon against each other. That is, neither of us tries to win an argument or get our way by appearing more spiritually correct than the other. Honesty also means an open sharing of doubts, struggles, and aspirations about our Christian walk. We believe that only in a relationship where you are free to be what you are will you have the nurturing context necessary to become what God wants you to be.

With shared spiritual goals in the context of an honest relationship, we discover new dimensions of life as we probe our faith and strive to strengthen each other. We have helped each other with such matters as how to maintain Christian integrity and witness in a secular university and how to love someone who is amoral and also your boss. With many experiences of mutual edification behind us, we look forward with anticipation to our coming spiritual discoveries.

ROBERT AND JEANETTE LAUER

- Give an example of a time when your partner's apology was an encouragement to you.
- Talk about how the two of you deal with apologies. Do you have your own unique styles of saying "I'm sorry"?
- Sometimes a person will offer a premature apology— without true sorrow—just to put an end to discomfort. Have you ever been caught in this trap? How can you avoid it?
- How can the two of you more effectively pursue the habit of humility in your marriage? Be specific.

❧ Soul to Soul

To deepen your spiritual intimacy this next week, make note of:

- What you gained from this session together.
- A pressure point in your partner's upcoming week you will pray about.
- A concrete kindness you can offer your partner this week.

❧ Prayer

O God of grace, overcome the darkness of our indifference with your light. Swap our pride with your humility. Exchange our self-interest with a genuine empathy for each other, and a spirit that seeks to understand our partner's point of view. May the peace that accompanies this kind of humility fill our hearts all week long. Amen.

Session Twenty-Three:
When Stress Strikes Your Marriage

It is 7:00 A.M., the start of another working day. Bleary-eyed from too little sleep, you drink a cup of coffee on your way out the door. Suddenly you remember that this evening it is your turn to host a couple's Bible study, so you frantically try to straighten up the house. You leave a few dishes in the sink and jump into your car to join the rest of the workforce in rush hour traffic. Ten minutes into your commute, however, you realize that the report you worked on last night is still on your nightstand. You have no option but to drive back and retrieve it.

Late for work, you open your office door and find the boss pacing inside. Your report was due an hour ago, you are told; the client is furious. Your heart begins to race. Your palms begin to sweat. And you would like nothing more than to run away.

Instead, you swallow the primal urge and try to explain yourself. Your boss grabs the report from your outstretched hand. "This better not happen again," he warns. You slump into your chair and fumble through the bottom drawer of your desk for a bottle of aspirin. Your stomach is churning, your back muscles knotting, your blood pressure climbing.

This stress response is the same experience our ancestors had when suddenly faced with a saber-toothed tiger—a pounding heart, tense muscles, and a desperate urge to fight or flee. And while the ancient threat of a hungry tiger may be gone, the modern jungle is no less perilous.

And since fighting or fleeing is not really an option in the civilized world, our body's natural reaction to stress has no outlet. As a result we suffer from ulcers, high blood pressure, and other physical symptoms. But that's not all. We carry the stress of the workaday world into our marriage. The fight-or-flight response, if not properly managed, creates tension in our partnership. If we can't take out our anger on the boss, for example, we might take it out on our spouse.

So what do we do? Extinguish all stress? No. Too little stress can be just as damaging as too much. The ideal goal is balance. Somewhere between the fight-or-flight spasms of too much tension and the dullness of too little, the challenge for each person and each couple is to find the level of manageable stress that invigorates life instead of ravaging it. Physical activity and calming techniques help a lot. But the only sure way to prevent your stress from becoming debilitating is to respond to the call of Christ when he says, "Come to me, . . . and I will give you rest" (Matt. 11:28). From the very beginning, rest has had a special significance for God: "And God blessed the seventh day and made it holy, because on it he rested" (Gen. 2:3).

The most frequently overlooked dimension in stress management, even among Christians, is resting in God's presence. This is not always easy, mind you. Even the great leader Moses had difficulty with it. He experienced unrelieved stress trying to keep two million Israelites happy as they wandered in the wilderness. In exasperation, Moses turned to God, pleading: "Why have you brought this trouble on your servant? . . . I cannot carry all these people by myself; the burden is too heavy for me." But God called Moses to rest in God's wisdom and soon his burden and his stress became more manageable (see Num. 11:11–17). The same God who called Moses to rest calls you and your partner to relax with each other in his peace.

FROM GOD'S WORD

Do not be anxious about anything, but in everything, by prayer and petition, with thanksgiving, present your requests to God. And the peace of God, which transcends all understanding, will guard your hearts and your minds in Christ Jesus.

PHILIPPIANS 4:6–7 ❧

❧ Your Turn

- What are you anxious about? Are you able to present it to God? If not, why not?
- Talk about how the two of you relax as individuals. What do each of you do to manage stress?
- Give an example of a recent stress outside your marriage that placed tension in your relationship. How does this happen and what can you do to diminish it?
- Discuss the current pace of your lives. If you are like most people, you are often stressed, out. What can you do this week to slow down?
- What is one thing you can each do for the other that will alleviate stress?

❧ Soul to Soul

To deepen your spiritual intimacy this next week, make note of:

- What you gained from this session together.
- A pressure point in your partner's upcoming week you will pray about.
- A concrete kindness you can offer your partner this week.

REAL-LIFE SOUL MATES

Our marriage in many respects has been "against all odds," but we wouldn't trade it for the world. We met in the fall of our first year in college and married as second, semester freshmen—just kids of eighteen and twenty. With little money but a lot of love, we ventured out on our own. Through the good times and bad we have learned some lessons about cultivating spiritual intimacy.

We both attended college full-time and worked nearly full-time early on in our marriage. We didn't have much time together. As a result, we almost did not make it through our early years of marriage. We both believe that spending time together, in quantity, is critical. Giving one another undivided attention in a relaxed atmosphere is crucial if heartfelt thoughts, desires, dreams, and feelings are to surface. We believe that it is only through this type of interaction and communication that growth as a couple can be attained.

We have also learned to believe in each other—above everyone else in the world. Knowing that someone, your best friend, will support you when life gets very tough and difficult provides a lot of encouragement and stability in life. We believe it only comes as a result of building on your commitment and stability in life. We are not to put each other down.

TIM AND JULIE CLINTON

Prayer

Lord God, you invited us to come to you to find rest. Help us together to still and quiet our souls in your presence. Grant us the wisdom to find a balanced lifestyle of challenge and rest that invigorates each of us without robbing us of joy. Amen.

SESSION TWENTY-FOUR:

DESPERATELY SEEKING
SCRIPTURE

We must have forty or fifty Bibles. They are of all sizes and colors—the *King James*, the *New King James*, the *Good News*, the *New American Standard*, the *Amplified*, the *Living*, the *Message*, the *New International Version*, the *New Revised Standard Bible*, and on and on. And then we have the workbook editions, the pocket editions, the illustrated editions, and the devotional editions. We are especially fond of the *NIV Couples' Devotional Bible*. Most of these, most of the time, however, sit on a shelf in our study at home.

But there are two Bibles—our personal Bibles—that are very different. Mine is a simple NIV with a brown leather cover that, because of wear, is no longer affixed to the spine (Les gave it to me on December 14, 1979—our first Christmas as a dating couple). His is a bigger, black leather Thompson Chain Reference NIV with thumb indentions for quick reference. Hardly a day goes by when these familiar books go unopened.

How about you? Do you make time to study God's Word? Have you discovered the beauty of Bible reading? One of the best descriptions of the Bible we have ever read came from old-time evangelist and professional baseball player Billy Sunday. In *Standing on the Rock*, he talked about entering the "wonderful temple" of the Bible:

> I entered at the portico of Genesis, walked down
> through the Old Testament art galleries, where pictures of

Noah, Abraham, Moses, Joseph, Isaac, Jacob, and Daniel hung on the wall. I passed into the music room of Psalms, where the Spirit swept the key-board of nature until it seemed that every reed and pipe in God's great organ responded to the tuneful harp of David, the sweet singer of Israel. I entered the chamber of Ecclesiastes, where the voice of the preacher was heard; and into the conservatory of Sharon, where the Lily of the Valley's sweet-scented spices filled and perfumed my life. I entered the business office of Proverbs, and then into the observatory room of the Prophets, where I saw telescopes of various sizes, pointed to far-off events, but all concentrated upon the bright and morning star.

I entered the audience room of the King of Kings, and caught a vision of His glory from the standpoint of Matthew, Mark, Luke, and John, passed into the Acts of the Apostles, where the Holy Spirit was doing His work in the formation of the infant church. Then into the correspondence room, where sat Paul, Peter, James, and John, penning their epistles. I stepped into the throne room of Revelation, where towered the glittering peaks, and got a vision of the King sitting upon the throne in all His glory, and I cried:

"All hail the power of Jesus' name,
Let angels prostrate fall,
Bring forth the royal diadem,
And crown him Lord of all."

If you and your partner read the Bible individually, on your own throughout each week, your souls will be nourished and your marriage will be blessed (see Ps. 19:11; Matt. 7:24; Luke 11:28; John 5:24; 8:31; Rev. 1:3). For you will have the Word of God written on your hearts (see Deut. 6:6; Ps. 119:11).

FROM GOD'S WORD

Let the word of Christ dwell in you richly as you teach and admonish one another with all wisdom, and as you sing psalms, hymns and spiritual songs with gratitude in your hearts to God.

COLOSSIANS 3:16 ❧

❧ Your Turn

- Many people feel guilty for not spending more time in reading the Bible. Do you ever struggle with consistent study of the Scripture?
- Does Bible study come more naturally to one of you than the other? This is not uncommon. What can you do to learn from each other?
- We all have our own devotional style. Describe to your partner how you go about your personal study time in the Word.
- Give an example of a time when Scripture encouraged or influenced you at a critical point in your life.
- How has your marriage been blessed and nourished by reading the Word of God?

❧ Soul to Soul

To deepen your spiritual intimacy this next week, make note of:

- What you gained from this session together.
- A pressure point in your partner's upcoming week you will pray about.
- A concrete kindness you can offer your partner this week.

REAL-LIFE SOUL MATES

Because Cathy and I were Christians when we married, we simply expected spiritual growth and spiritual intimacy to happen easily. How wrong we were! We tried the "roller coaster" devotional method for several years, and our daily devotions gradually shifted to a few times a month. Reading books together promised to change the situation, but we never made it through even one. We felt guilty that we weren't growing together. We were better at discipling teenagers in the youth group than we were at discipling each other.

Then we finally developed a spiritual tool that works for us. We call it "Jim and Cathy's weekly meeting." Although we pray with our children daily and with each other more than weekly, this weekly meeting has become the cornerstone for our spiritual intimacy as a couple. It's simple. We enjoy our devotional time for the week; we share our greatest joy, our greatest struggle, an affirmation, a wish or hope, and physical goals; we pray; and we discuss a book of the month. There are days when this takes us fifteen minutes, but we have also had marathon meetings for three hours.

JIM AND CATHY BURNS

✺ Prayer

Our Savior, you have given us your Word as our resource for life. Your Word revives our souls. It improves our wisdom, gives us joy, and fills our minds with greater light. May our marriage reap the great rewards promised for those who study and live by your Word. Thank you for the marvelous gift of Scripture. Amen.

Session Twenty-Five:
Help! We Need Somebody!

Chances are that just this week you and your partner had a situation that required negotiation and compromise—a money matter came up, a conflict in household chores arose, or a discrepancy over discretionary time raised its head. And chances are that you quickly worked out a solution.

But truth be known, you and your spouse might encounter issues that aren't easily solved. Some stubborn problems come up time and again which you won't be able to work out on your own. And chances are, sooner or later, you'll need outside help to reach a resolution. So if that time arises, be ready. Make a commitment to each other now that you will seek the necessary help when you need it.

Oh, we know it never feels good to ask someone else for help. But seeking counsel is never a sign of weakness. Proverbs affirms this kind of help again and again: "Let the wise listen and add to their learning, and let the discerning get guidance" (1:5); "Plans fail for lack of counsel, but with many advisors they succeed" (15:22); "Instruct a wise man and he will be wiser still; teach a righteous man and he will add to his learning" (9:9).

Maybe you are thinking that you will never need a counselor because God can speak directly to you. That's true. But more often than not, God counsels us through the wisdom of other people, individuals who are wise, gifted, and trained to administer his healing.

How do you know when it is time to turn to a sensitive pastor or a professional counselor? Our friend Everett Worthington, in *Hope for Troubled Marriages*, lists several situations which indicate that a couple should consider seeing a counselor. Here are a few from his list: You are locked in a power struggle, someone is deeply depressed, alcohol or drug dependency has entered the marriage, sexual difficulties (impotence or premature ejaculation) have become a strain on the relationship, someone is suffering damage to self-esteem, either of you is unable to forgive a past transgression, commitment to the marriage is wearing thin, your marital tensions are snowballing quickly. These are just a few of the indicators Everett notes. The bottom line is that if you think you need marriage counseling you probably do.

What should you look for in a good counselor? If the counselor is not your pastor, we suggest that you explore his or her beliefs and values (are they in sync with yours?). You will also want to know about the counselor's training and education. But one of the most important things to do in finding a competent counselor is to get a good referral. Ask around. Word of mouth is often the best way to find someone who will really help.

Chances are that you are doing a pretty good job of solving your problems yourselves. But if the time comes when you need something more, remember that while Christ is the ultimate Counselor (see Isa. 9:6), the servants of Christ that work in counseling offices and pastor's studies are often a conduit for administering his help. So "listen to advice and accept instruction, and in the end you will be wise" (Prov. 19:20).

FROM GOD'S WORD

But the Counselor, the Holy Spirit, whom the Father will send to you in my name, will teach you all things and will remind you of everything I have said to you.

JOHN 14:26

REAL-LIFE SOUL MATES

Spiritual intimacy was always a goal in our marriage, but we didn't realize its importance until our marriage was in its adolescence. We came to Christ as adults. In fact, we committed our lives the same night, in the same service. That step, however, did not assure spiritual intimacy.

As we look back over our marriage, we realize that the depth of openness and honesty we share today began to develop when we finally were able to really risk vulnerability with each other. We attribute the retarded development to two factors: First, Norm's career as an NFL offensive lineman for fourteen years set the stage for him to fulfill the role of "macho man." His father was strong, silent, and in charge. Failures and weaknesses were not acknowledged or discussed. Second, Bobbie grew up in an alcoholic home and determined that her own family would be different. Early in marriage she adopted the role of a Christian wife described for her. She knew how to ignore feelings, misgivings, and warning signs, as she had growing up in a dysfunctional family.

Married and established in our roles, we assumed that intimacy would be a by-product of living together. This, however, was not the case. Two people can spend their entire adulthood together and never develop intimacy. To accomplish it, we had to set aside roles and expectations. Our intent is to be honest and open with one another—and to extend to one another the same grace and mercy that Christ has extended to us. We determined never to abuse the trust and vulnerability of the other. We liken this to our relationship with God as a kind Father who would never ridicule, betray, or abuse his precious children. This is also how we develop spiritual intimacy with God! What a concept—to offer to each other what he offers to us!

NORM AND BOBBIE EVANS

118

❧ Your Turn

- Why is seeking guidance so crucial to acquiring the wisdom that leads to a fulfilled life?
- Give an example of a time when advice, insight, or counsel from a trusted source facilitated growth in you or your marriage relationship.
- Identify an experienced, healthy couple you might invite to mentor you as a couple. What do you think about this idea?
- Take an inventory of your relationship. Are there any red flags that might alert you to the need for marriage counseling? How can you be sure you are being honest about your real needs?
- What can you do in a concrete way to ensure that you will seek help if and when it is necessary for your marriage?

❧ Soul to Soul

To deepen your spiritual intimacy this next week, make note of:
- What you gained from this session together.
- A pressure point in your partner's upcoming week you will pray about.
- A concrete kindness you can offer your partner this week.

❧ Prayer

Our Father, we recognize our need for help. Give us teachable spirits and keep us sensitive to the counsel of your Holy Spirit. And save us from the fear of seeking special help from qualified people when we need it. Thank you for your great love. Amen.

❧

SESSION TWENTY-SIX:
FIGHTING THE GOOD FIGHT

Conflict is a natural component of every marriage. No matter how deeply a man and woman love each other, they will encounter conflict. Thirty-seven percent of newlyweds admit to being more critical of their mates after marriage. And thirty percent report an increase in arguments after the honeymoon.

Whether you argue does not determine the health of your marriage. Far more important than how often you argue is *how* you argue. Dr. John Gottman of the University of Washington has been studying marriages for more than twenty years and he has identified the signs in conflict that almost always spell disaster. He calls them "The Four Horsemen of the Apocalypse." And when they gallop into your relationship, danger is imminent. In a continuum from least to most dangerous, the four horsemen are: criticism, contempt, defensiveness, and stonewalling.

Do these characteristics describe your quarrels? Be on the lookout. Criticism, of course, often comes into play in marital spats, but when it leads to contempt—when sarcasm and name-calling enter the picture—you are on a slippery slope. At the risk of oversimplifying Gottman's findings, you might think of a destructive argument as one that resorts to belittling and degrading. When this happens, partners begin to focus on every past sin and failure of their spouse and aggressively whittle away at each other's dignity. This kind of arguing drives a wedge between couples. The next time they argue, the wedge will be driven farther and the division in their relationship made more wide. After enough shouting matches the pattern becomes ingrained and is likely to be settled ultimately in a divorce court.

To avoid the deadly trap of contempt, focus on the issue at hand—not your partner's character. If the problem is in-laws, for example, or how money is spent, or the use of personal time, argue about *that*, and stay away from personality assassination. You may disagree vehemently, but don't shut your partner out; don't roll your eyes in disgust. Stay on the issue and God will grant you patience and encouragement in a spirit of unity (see Rom. 15:5).

We'll say it again: Conflict is a natural part of building intimacy. So don't avoid differences. Don't bury your conflicts. Go ahead, fight. But keep your conflict restricted to the issues that really matter.

You've probably seen the "grant me the wisdom to accept the things I cannot change" prayer on plaques and posters. It may be trivialized by overfamiliarity, but it's true: One of the major tasks of marriage is learning what can and should be changed (habits of nagging, for example) and what should be overlooked (the fact that your in-laws are coming for Christmas). So remember this saying from Proverbs: "Reckless words pierce like a sword, but the tongue of the wise brings healing" (12:18).

FROM GOD'S WORD

You have heard that it was said to the people long ago, "Do not murder, and anyone who murders will be subject to judgment." But I tell you that anyone who is angry with his brother will be subject to judgment. Again, anyone who says to his brother, 'Raca,' [an Aramaic term of contempt] is answerable to the Sanhedrin. But anyone who says, 'You fool!' will be in danger of the fire of hell.

Therefore, if you are offering your gift at the altar and there remember that your brother has something against you, leave your gift there in front of the altar. First go and be reconciled to your brother; then come and offer your gift.

MATTHEW 5:21–24

REAL-LIFE SOUL MATES

This morning we had an argument. It was our special time in the morning when we sit down to talk and communicate, but there we were arguing. Instead of allowing it to escalate, we stopped and began to process what was happening.

Marriage for us can be pictured as walking through life hand in hand trying to keep in step with each other. It wasn't easy to learn to walk in step, and even after being married for twenty-five years there are still times we find ourselves slightly out of step and needing to check out why.

Several things happen when you're trying to walk in step. When one of us takes a step in a different direction, we are drawn up short and have to decide what is happening. Which way do we go? Who decides? Is this a direction we both should go or do we need to continue in the original path? There are days when it's easy to say or think, "I'm tired of staying in step." But it is a commitment, based on the solid belief that we must make adjustments as we walk together.

Naturally there are times when we do need to evaluate the direction of our path. For example, after serving as short-term missionaries for two years, Joyce was ready to go home. She assumed we would resume "normal" life, since living in the Amazon jungle was far from where she grew up in Chicago. However, it was hard to ignore the direction God was gradually leading us: to serve full-time in Bible translation. At that point we agreed that, if indeed this was the direction God was guiding us, we would take some steps in that direction and see if the doors would open. We took some very hesitant steps at that time, but when God confirmed our path, step by step, we felt confident this was the direction for our lives. We have recognized that walking together combines the best of our abilities and allows us to serve the Lord more effectively.

KEN AND JOYCE PRETTOL

❧ Your Turn

- Discuss the meaning of Christ's warning about the destructiveness of contempt in relationships. Why would he mention this?
- Give an example of a time when a disagreement strengthened your marriage—a time you were strengthened because of your honest admission of conflict.
- What have been your models for learning how to resolve conflicts? How did your parents fight?
- When it comes to difficult issues, what are the roles each of you tend to take and how can you learn from the strengths of the other?
- How can the two of you prepare in advance to make your next conflict a "good fight"? Talk about this in specific terms.

❧ Soul to Soul

To deepen your spiritual intimacy this next week, make note of:

- What you gained from this session together.
- A pressure point in your partner's upcoming week you will pray about.
- A concrete kindness you can offer your partner this week.

❧ Prayer

Teach us, O Lord, to disagree without a critical or contemptuous spirit. Lift us above the fear of conflict and allow our differences to strengthen one another as iron sharpens iron. Help us never to lose sight of our partner's true significance even in the shadow of disagreement. Bind us together through Jesus Christ our Lord. Amen.

❧

Session Twenty-Seven:
A Kiss on the Lips

Rebecca and Steve, very much in love, had been married only a few weeks when she cooked eggplant lasagna. She asked Steve if he liked it. Steve knew Rebecca had worked hard to make it and was afraid that he would offend her if he was honest. "Oh yes," he told Rebecca, "it's great!" But he hated it. Believing that Steve really liked it, Rebecca began cooking the dish quite regularly. Since she had difficulty breaking down the recipe, there was always a great quantity of leftovers, so the lasagna appeared many times during the week. Finally Steve could bear it no longer and, in a moment of anger, he confessed that he hated her cooking, that it gagged him, that he never wanted to see that eggplant lasagna on his table again! Rebecca was shocked and hurt. He had *lied* to her. In tears she said, "I'll never believe you again!"

The tragedy of most seemingly insignificant experiences of deception is that they grow, and ultimately cast a shadow of distrust over a relationship. That's why Solomon wrote, "An honest answer is like a kiss on the lips" (Prov. 24:26).

Soul mates must have integrity. Without it, Scripture says, we will be despised and destroyed (see Ps. 5:6; 63:11; 101:7; Prov. 11:3; 12:8; 19:1; Rev. 21:8). Integrity means telling the truth, keeping our promises, doing what we said we would do, choosing to be accountable, and taking as our motto *semper fidelis*—the promise to be *always faithful*.

"If I *always* tell the truth," you may be saying, "won't I hurt my partner's feelings?" No. Truth is "brutal" only when it is a partial truth or when it is meant to cause pain. If, for example, Leslie asks me if I like the banana bread she made, I could say, "Yuck! I can't stand it." But would that be the truth? Only part of it. It would be more completely honest to say, "Not really, I've never liked banana bread—but it doesn't make a bit of difference to me, this meal is still good." When Paul wrote to the church he began in Thessalonica (Acts 17:1–9) he said, "For the appeal we make does not spring from error or impure motives, nor are we trying to trick you. On the contrary, we speak as men approved by God to be entrusted with the gospel. We are not trying to please men but God, who tests our hearts" (1 Thess. 2:3–4). That is the key to "speaking the truth in love" (Eph. 4:15)—not to trick or manipulate, but to love our spouse and to please God.

Honesty, as a popular song says, is such a lonely word. At times it does seem that everyone is so untrue. And it's been that way for a long time. Consider these verses: "All men are liars" (Ps. 116:11); "Friend deceives friend, and no one speaks the truth" (Jer. 9:5). The book of Proverbs asks, "Many a man claims to have unfailing love, but a faithful man who can find?" (20:6). The gift of integrity is so rare. But doesn't your marriage deserve it?

So kiss your spouse on the lips with honesty. He or she will say with the psalmist, "The law from your mouth is more precious to me than thousands of pieces of silver and gold" (119:72).

FROM GOD'S WORD

Therefore, since through God's mercy we have this ministry, we do not lose heart. Rather, we have renounced secret and shameful ways; we do not use deception, nor do we distort the word of God. On the contrary, by setting forth the truth plainly we commend ourselves to every man's conscience in the sight of God.

2 CORINTHIANS 4:1–2

REAL-LIFE SOUL MATES

Marital intimacy is the way two people weave oneness into their relationship. Nothing has enabled this more than our unconditional commitment to stay married, which has empowered us to disagree without coming unglued or threatening separation. In fact, we became more one as we saw the brawn of our commitment in the midst of strong disagreements. No matter what comes between us, there is never a question that we will stay with it, that we can and will work through it, and that we will be better off because of it.

This unconditional commitment also keeps us spending time together, almost 16,000 days so far. Most of these days were ordinary days, but in the mix were some personal, spiritual highs never to be forgotten. Most of these stemmed from the afterglow of hard, tiring, or frantic times. Once, driving home dog-tired in a hot car, we watched the big, West Texas sunset cast its pale gold and purple magic over us. That moment was supernatural for both of us—we both just turned and gazed into each other's eyes—no words needed or uttered. It was total intimacy. We were secure with each other and deep in the pleasure of the presence of God. How long we were mesmerized I don't know, but we both felt an intense oneness, dispensed by all the years we had lovingly "banked" our mutual commitment to God and our children.

We have had many of those special days, some trying, some rewarding. But as we reflect on our most intimate times, they come more frequently from victories over frantic, even desperate times. That is the message of the Cross as well. Anyone can stay in a relationship when everything is "good, better, or best." But it is our opinion that the bad days—rightly committed to—convey more intimacy into the marriage than the good days.

PAUL AND GLADYS FAULKNER

❧ Your Turn

- In your opinion, why is truth so fundamental to love? Can you have love without truth?
- How have you struggled with being truthful (a desire to protect, a propensity to exaggerate, a tendency to control or to avoid a conflict, etc.)?
- Give an example of a time when you benefited from an honest, if yet painful, answer from someone? How did it help you?
- What experiences have you shared that have strengthened and developed the trust between you?
- How can you work together more effectively to "speak the truth in love"?

❧ Soul to Soul

To deepen your spiritual intimacy this next week, make note of:

- What you gained from this session together.
- A pressure point in your partner's upcoming week you will pray about.
- A concrete kindness you can offer your partner this week.

❧ Prayer

Gracious God, help us to give ourselves to the task of developing personal integrity—especially in all our ordinary conversations this week. Teach us how to be honest without hurting anyone. Release us from the compulsion to trick, manipulate, or protect our spouse from the truth. Amen.

SESSION TWENTY-EIGHT:
HOW IRON SHARPENS IRON

When researchers asked husbands and wives, "What is it you've gotten out of marriage?" couples often said something like, "My partner has shown me parts of my personality I didn't know were there." In other words, marriage heightened my self-awareness and has helped me to grow.

Personal growth is one of the fringe benefits of a good marriage. Having a spouse, in a sense, is like having an intimate mirror that reflects who you really are and, as a result, provides more opportunities for personal change. That's why research shows that married people are healthier on nearly every spectrum than the rest of the population. That is also why Scripture says, "He [or she] who finds a wife [or husband] finds what is good and receives favor from the LORD" (Prov. 18:22).

Marriage comes with a built-in reality check. We ask questions of our partner like, "Do you think I came across too flippant when John asked me about my job?" Or, "Do you think I don't smile very much?" And sometimes our partner says things like, "Honey, you do tend to jump to conclusions at times." Or "Do you realize how much you worry about that?" Questions and comments like these emerge naturally in a healthy marriage, and they become the stimulus for personal change.

Everyone needs to grow. No one has become all he or she can. Even the apostle Paul said, "Not that I have already obtained all this, or have already been made perfect, but I press on to take hold of that for which Christ Jesus took hold of me" (Phil. 3:12).

Of course, change isn't easy. Take the configuration of the letters on a computer keyboard as an illustration. Back in the 1870s, a manufacturer of typewriters received complaints about the typewriter keys sticking together if the user went too fast. Engineers for the company decided that the best way to keep the keys from jamming was to slow the operator down. So they developed a more inefficient keyboard with letters like "O" and "I" (two of the most frequently used letters in the alphabet) positioned for the relatively weaker ring and little fingers. Depressing these keys simply took more time. The problem was solved, no more jammed keys. Since the time of that solution, however, typing technology and word processing have advanced significantly. Today's electric typewriters and word processors can go much faster than any human can type. The problem is that we don't want to change the keyboard—even though it would help us type faster.

Change is hard. But don't allow that to stand in the way of pinpointing something you need to change about yourself. Ask for feedback from your spouse and, with his or her help, devise a personal plan for improvement. You and your partner can help each other become self-aware and your marriage will be the better for it. "As iron sharpens iron," Proverbs says, "so one [person] sharpens another" (27:17).

From God's Word

And he said: "I tell you the truth, unless you change and become like little children, you will never enter the kingdom of heaven. Therefore, whoever humbles himself like this child is the greatest in the kingdom of heaven."

MATTHEW 18:3–4

REAL-LIFE SOUL MATES

One of the most important sources of spiritual intimacy for Janie and me is the cultivation of our intellectual compatibility through reading. It is our habit to read a book and then pass it on to the other for comment and discussion.

When I'm traveling or away for any period of time we both read the same paperback and then we can discuss it on the telephone while I'm away and upon my return. This keeps us on the same page, as it were, of our own story. We cover the waterfront in our selection, from serious Christian reading to classical devotions to mystery novels. This way we are dealing with the world of ideas, character development, tragedy, mobility, sin and its consequences, inspirational models, great events, accomplishments, and even suffering and death.

Almost all articles, books, and discussions of good marriages include the word *communication*. Communication about what? If the topic is simply the details of running a household, all relationships can be perfunctory, even boring and something to avoid, just another detail in an already full life.

For us reading is an enriching experience and informs our response to our responsibilities, friends, and daily challenges. Over the years I've noticed many couples who experience intellectual drift as one "outgrows" the other in their chosen vocational field. Meeting each other intellectually on common intellectual ground is a deterrent to this pitfall and, incidentally, it is an aid to intimacy as well. With so much emphasis on human sexuality, it is wise to acknowledge that the most important sexual organ is in the head: Nothing else works without it.

JAY AND JANIE KESLER

❧ Your Turn

- How do you incorporate the process of personal change into your spiritual pilgrimage? How does God speak to you about things you need to change?
- Has being married increased your level of self-awareness? In what ways?
- Share with your partner the desires you have for personal improvement?
- Give an example of a time when your partner's feedback helped produce a positive change in you.
- What can you do to more effectively promote growth in one another? In other words, how can you "sharpen" each other?

❧ Soul to Soul

To deepen your spiritual intimacy this next week, make note of:

- What you gained from this session together.
- A pressure point in your partner's upcoming week you will pray about.
- A concrete kindness you can offer your partner this week.

❧ Prayer

Our Father in heaven, grant unto us the courage, grace, and strength to look into the mirror of our partner's eyes and listen attentively to his or her speech, so we may clearly understand the ways we may improve our side of the relationship. Complete your work in us so that we reflect your image. Amen.

❧

SESSION TWENTY-NINE:

THE IMPORTANCE OF SAYING "I LOVE YOU"

Emily sat in our office weeping. She came for counseling on her own, without telling her husband. "I am so hungry for affection," she confided in us. "We have been married for twenty-five years, and I know he is capable of tenderness. He shows it to the dog. But..." Emily's voice broke down and her tears began to flow. She reached for a tissue and quietly said, "...I'd just like to hear him say 'I love you.'"

Three simple words. So critical to marriage. We take these tender words for granted sometimes, but we have never known anyone who got tired of hearing "I love you" ... before leaving the house in the morning ... after a quick message on the answering machine ... while working in the garden ... before dozing off in bed. These little words are like nutrients to a marriage. Without a consistent dose of verbal expression, without saying and hearing those words, the soul of a marriage withers.

Think about it. We have over six hundred thousand words in the English language and more synonyms per word than are found in any other language. However, we have only one word with which to express all the various shadings of love. Deficient as English is in this respect, we long to hear the familiar words, "I love you."

Again and again, your spouse needs to hear the words. And, by the way, it is just as important for you to say them. At the university where we work there is a sophisticated voice mail system on our phones. One of the features is called "future delivery." It enables a person to record a message to someone and then specify the time and date they want the message delivered. One day I (Les) got the idea of sending Leslie several "I love you" messages on her phone. "Why not do a bunch of them now while I'm thinking about it," I thought to myself. As a Type-A, I was excited to be so loving and check it off my to-do list at the same time. So I recorded my tender messages one after the next and then sent them "future delivery" on different days throughout the coming month. Leslie, not knowing what I had done, believed she was receiving spontaneous, loving messages from her husband every few days. And all I had to do was sit back and let my voice mail do my romancing. Funny thing, however. While Leslie, none the wiser, loved my messages, I began to feel phony. Saying "I love you," for me, was starting to fall into the same category as paying the bills. Well, needless to say, I haven't put my love on "future delivery" since. My sneaky scheme, however, taught me something important—I need to say "I love you" as much as Leslie needs to hear it.

The poet W. H. Auden remarked, "We must love one another or die!" He is surely right. A marriage cannot survive without verbal expressions of love. So pray that the Lord will "make your love increase and overflow for each other" (1 Thess. 3:12).

FROM GOD'S WORD

Love is patient, love is kind. It does not envy, it does not boast, it is not proud. It is not rude, it is not self-seeking, it is not easily angered, it keeps no record of wrongs. Love does not delight in evil but rejoices with the truth. It always protects, always trusts, always hopes, always perseveres. Love never fails.

1 CORINTHIANS 13:4–8

REAL-LIFE SOUL MATES

Intimacy is about sharing all of life together. It is like unlocking all of the doors of who you are. There are no secrets. Privacy may be granted but is never protected as a right.

Since we grew up together and started dating in high school, we have known each other very well for all of our lives. But we have worked at keeping up-to-date. Intimacy has a short shelf life.

Every morning we talk to each other about plans for the day. Often we have prayed through each other's schedule. Whenever possible we call each other during the day for a minute or more of sharing. Sometimes it is only to say "I love you!" If the other doesn't answer, a message of hello and love is left on voice mail. We have often stopped by each other's places of work during the day. When Charleen was a bank teller, Leith drove by her drive-up window. Charleen often stops by Leith's office days in a row. At night we review all the day held. It has no feeling of reporting or accountability, but sharing of genuine interest in each other.

Perhaps the best times have been early in the morning before the phone rings or children are up. We each pray, often holding hands as we talk to God. We sense that all of life is open and known to God and each other, and we enjoy knowing that the partnership is three-way.

When the crises of life have come they have been surrounded with hours of talking them through. We have prayed together often. Sometimes it is not both taking a turn but one blessing the other. When his father died Leith cried and Charleen held him and prayed for him and blessed him.

It isn't so much that there is a piece of our relationship that is spiritual or that is intimate. All of life is deliberately shared with each other and with God.

LEITH AND CHARLEEN ANDERSON

๕ Your Turn

- How do you make your love "overflow" for each other? Does your faith influence your expressions of love?
- How was love expressed in your family while growing up? How often were the words "I love you" used?
- Is it more difficult for one or both of you to express loving words routinely? Why or why not?
- Tell about a recent incident when you were especially appreciative of your partner saying "I love you."
- What can you and your partner do to cultivate a free exchange of loving messages in your relationship?

๕ Soul to Soul

To deepen your spiritual intimacy this next week, make note of:

- What you gained from this session together.
- A pressure point in your partner's upcoming week you will pray about.
- A concrete kindness you can offer your partner this week.

๕ Prayer

O God, our Father, teach us to open the doors to tenderness by freely saying to each other, "I love you." Open our mouths, unstop our ears, and illumine our eyes to the many ways we can be healing reminders of your love to one another. May loving words fill our home and empower our marriage. Amen.

Session Thirty:
In Sickness and In Health

Leslie had the flu a couple of days ago. I can't stand it when she's sick. I feel so helpless, like I can't do a thing in the world to make her feel any better. I run to the store and pick up a bottle of 7-Up and some soda crackers. This last time I bought a couple of different kinds of flu medicine. "That's so sweet," she said to me as she sat up on the couch wrapped in a blanket.

Okay, I thought to myself, *it will be another day or so and she'll be up and at 'em*. But she wasn't. For the rest of the week she stayed in bed, sipping 7-Up from a straw and complaining that the house was too cold, then too hot, then too cold. *What am I supposed to do now?* I wondered. I called our doctor. He said the flu was going around and all Leslie needed was bed rest. Urgh! I wanted to *do* something so I wouldn't feel so helpless. I guess that's why I enjoy stories of couples whose love has survived a time of serious illness. And I'm a sucker for any movie about tragic love.

But there is one real-life love story that invades my mind whenever Leslie gets sick. It puts my feelings of helplessness into perspective. In *Saving Your Marriage Before It Starts*, we told the story of Robertson McQuilkin and his wife Muriel, and it deserves repeating. The love he demonstrated for her when she was diagnosed with Alzheimer's disease is nothing less than extraordinary. Robertson was a college president who still had eight years to go before retirement. Muriel, once the host of a successful radio program, was experiencing tragic memory failure. She could not speak in sentences, only words, and often words that made little sense. But she could say one sentence, and she said it often: "I love you." While Robertson's friends urged him to arrange for the institutionalization of Muriel, he would not stand for it. *How could anyone love her the way I do?* asked Robertson.

Have you thought much about the part of your wedding vow that says, "To love and to honor in sickness and in health?" Robertson McQuilkin has. But not only has he thought about it, he's lived it.

Believing that being faithful to Muriel "in sickness and in health" was a matter of integrity, Robertson McQuilkin resigned his presidency to care for his wife full-time. Several years have passed since his resignation, and Muriel has steadily declined. She sits most of the time, while he writes. "She seems still to have affection for me," says Robertson. "What more could I ask? Daily, I discern new manifestations of the kind of person she is. I also see fresh manifestations of God's love—the God I long to love more fully."

Robertson understood the words of Christ when he said, "I needed clothes and you clothed me, I was sick and you looked after me" (Matt. 25:36). How about you? The next time your partner is ill remember that it is an opportunity to put hands and feet to your marriage vows—in sickness and in health.

From God's Word

Jesus went through Galilee, teaching in their synagogues, preaching the good news of the kingdom, and healing every disease and sickness among the people.

Matthew 4:23 ❧

❧ Your Turn

- Why do you think Christ so strongly identifies himself with the sick and needy?

REAL-LIFE SOUL MATES

Although Charlie requires round-the-clock nursing care because he is on life support, we work on finding windows of time to be alone. Usually at the end of the day, and many times into the wee hours of the morning, we talk, laugh, pray over the happenings of the day.

We face continuous battles every day. Many times we've prayed through tears and through feelings of helplessness and hopelessness. But God's Word has always prevailed, and we've found that any dilemma can be overcome with an attitude change and a heart full of prayer and constantly dying to self. We are still learning to be quick to ask each other for forgiveness for misunderstandings. And we are still learning to be even quicker to offer forgiveness. Isn't it sad how the smallest of disagreements can fracture a relationship?

We spend a lot of time reaching out to, and praying for, others who suffer, which helps to take the focus off of our own trials. We especially enjoy reading marriage relationship books together to bolster our perspectives.

A big part of our strength comes from our children, who share Scripture verses, prayers, and Christian books to strengthen us. We feel truly blessed even though by the world's standards our personal situation would be considered a tragedy.

CHARLIE AND LUCY WEDEMEYER

- What does "in sickness and in health" mean to you? How do you and will you live out this part of your marriage vow?
- Describe to your partner how you like to be treated when you are ill (doted on, left alone, etc.).
- How do you feel when your spouse is sick? Talk about the role of helping the sick partner. What is the toughest part?
- Give an example of a time when you were ill and the care of a parent or loved one was especially meaningful.

ᵎ Soul to Soul

To deepen your spiritual intimacy this next week, make note of:

- What you gained from this session together.
- A pressure point in your partner's upcoming week you will pray about.
- A concrete kindness you can offer your partner this week.

ᵎ Prayer

Gracious God, it is during the times when we are the most unlovable that you embrace us. Like the father of the prodigal son, you celebrate our presence with you even when we are covered with filth and desperately needy. Give us a gentle love and unfailing courage to be there for each other when things are worse, *not better. Amen.*

ᵎ

SESSION THIRTY-ONE:
THE POWER OF LOVE IN ACTION

We have some friends who have been married more than thirty years. In their mid-fifties now, they seem to enjoy all the blessings possible for a healthy married couple—a beautiful home, good friends, bright children, and fulfilling careers. But their marriage hasn't been a walk on easy street. Their second child, a boy, was just four years old when he wandered into a neighbor's yard and drowned in their swimming pool.

The mother found her son face down in the water and worked frantically to revive him, as did the emergency crew, but his life was lost. Faced with this tragedy and the unbearable grief that followed, this couple could have given up. After all, it is not uncommon for a marriage to dissolve in the face of overwhelming suffering. Strangely, sorrowful partners sometimes retreat to separate and bitter corners of misery. And because misery doesn't always love company, their circumstances tear them apart instead of bringing them together. But not this couple, they chose to call upon the power of love to help them weather their tragedy as partners.

Are you and your partner cultivating the power of love? We hope you will never be forced to test its strength, and we pray you will always rest in the courage that comes from a healthy Christian marriage. "Who shall separate us from the love of Christ? Shall trouble or hardship or persecution or famine or nakedness or danger or sword? . . . No, in all these things we are more than conquerors through him who loved us" (Rom. 8:35, 37).

In his book *Power Through Constructive Thinking*, Emmet Fox wrote these words about the power of love:

> There is no difficulty that enough love will not conquer; no disease that enough love will not heal; no door that enough love will not open; no gulf that enough love will not bridge; no wall that enough love will not throw down; no sin that enough love will not redeem.
>
> It makes no difference how deeply seated may be the trouble, how hopeless the outlook, how muddled the tangle, how great the mistake, a sufficient realization of love will dissolve it all. If only you could love enough you would be the happiest and most powerful being in the world.

What a marvelous resource partners can be to one another. For as we cultivate love we strengthen our ability to cope with all that life might bring. And in the process we are reminded that "in all things God works for the good of those who love him" (Rom. 8:28).

From God's Word

I pray that out of his glorious riches he may strengthen you with power through his Spirit in your inner being, so that Christ may dwell in your hearts through faith. And I pray that you, being rooted and established in love, may have power, together with all the saints to grasp how wide and long and high and deep is the love of Christ.

Ephesians 3:16–18 ❧

❧ Your Turn

- How do you experience the love of Christ in your life? When have you felt most loved by God?

REAL-LIFE SOUL MATES

The foundation upon which Steve and I established our marriage is the same today as it was when we pledged our covenant promise in the Spring of 1975. It is our individual commitment to our relationship with Christ that is our anchor in the midst of the storms of life. Realizing that most marital problems are simply spiritual problems that manifest themselves in the marriage, Steve and I seek to grow in the knowledge and grace of Christ. The closer we grow to him, the closer we grow to one another.

There are very practical ways in which our faith makes us better spouses. Believing and embracing what God has said about each other and our intrinsic value, for example, motivates us to treat one another with respect. If Steve is going to be late for dinner, he calls to tell me. When Steve is finished eating, he takes the dish to the sink. If he needs physical love and affirmation, even though I may not be in the mood, I give him the kind of love he needs. If I'm tired and need to be left alone, he gives me the space I need.

When the practical, everyday needs of a spouse are met, then the spiritual need for oneness is possible. We can't treat one another rudely and then expect to have a meaningful devotional time together. People aren't made that way.

To be great in the kingdom of God, we know we must be servants. The same is true in the simplest expression of that kingdom, the family. Consider this poem that hangs on our wall.

We believe a man and wife would have a better married life
If they would try out serving one another
For deeper love is felt when what is done is not for self
But when it's done to satisfy the other.

(© 1984 Steve Chapman)

STEVE AND ANNIE CHAPMAN

- Give a personal example of a time when an unexpected or painful blow was mitigated by love in your life.
- Since misery doesn't always love company, what can you do now to ensure that when misery strikes your lives you will not be pulled apart?
- What can you do as a couple to cultivate a reliance on the power of God's love in times of difficulty?
- Do you agree with Emmet Fox that no matter how deep the trouble, a sufficient realization of love will dissolve it? Why or why not?

❧ Soul to Soul

To deepen your spiritual intimacy this next week, make note of:

- What you gained from this session together.
- A pressure point in your partner's upcoming week you will pray about.
- A concrete kindness you can offer your partner this week.

❧ Prayer

Dear God, sometimes the storms of life threaten to overcome our human capacity to love. Help us to drive our roots down deep, to be so established in your love that we might know its height and depth which surpasses understanding and be filled to overflowing with a measure of that love within our marriage—especially in the face of unexpected loss, bitter disappointments, and unsolvable situations. Amen.

❧

SESSION THIRTY-TWO:
AVOIDING THE BLAME GAME

Have you noticed lately that everyone seems to be a victim? The media has. The *New Yorker* magazine, for example, recently featured a cover story with the title, "The New Culture of Victimization," and the headline of the inside story was "Don't Blame Me!" On the cover of a recent *Time* magazine these words appeared: "Cry Babies and Eternal Victims!" *Esquire* followed with an article titled "A Confederacy of Complainers." It seems people these days don't want to be held accountable.

Take, for example, the FBI agent who embezzled two thousand dollars from the government and lost it in an afternoon of gambling in Atlantic City. He was fired, as he should have been, but he won a reinstatement to his post when the court ruled that he had a gambling handicap and was thus protected under federal law.

Or consider the man who applied for a job as a park attendant in Dane County, Wisconsin. A background check revealed that he had been convicted more than thirty times for flashing and indecent exposure. But when the park service turned him down, he sued them. He had never flashed in a park, only in libraries and laundromats, and thus employment officials determined that he should be hired because he had been a victim of job discrimination.

We will leave it to the social commentators to explain just how our new culture of victimization will affect society, but we know exactly how it can affect a marriage. Once a husband or wife becomes wrapped up in the blame game (blaming parents, genes, a boss, or a spouse, for example), a vicious cycle of shirked responsibility permeates the relationship. Soon each partner is looking for ways to avoid responsibility and shift the blame. Of course, this is nothing new. Ever since Adam blamed Eve, and Eve blamed the serpent, we have learned the trick of finding excuses. Accused of wrongdoing, we respond, "Who me?" "I didn't do it," "It's only a game," "Well, you asked for it," or "I didn't mean to."

But let's be honest. We *are* responsible. As human beings with a free will we have choices and nobody makes them for us. While we are not necessarily the cause of all that happens in our lives, we are responsible for what we make of what happens. As Scripture says, "You, my brothers, were called to be free. But do not use your freedom to indulge the sinful nature; rather, serve one another in love" (Gal. 5:13).

Dr. Scott Peck, in his best-selling *The Road Less Traveled*, writes about the tendency unhealthy people have to give their free will away. "Sooner or later, if they are to be healed, they must learn that the entirety of one's adult life is a series of personal choices, decisions. If they can accept this totally, then they become free people. To the extent they do not accept this, they will forever feel themselves victims."

Don't let your marriage become a blame game. Don't lay the blame on your church, your parents, your schooling, your income, your siblings, your friends, your government, or anything else. Take responsibility for your feelings and your actions and watch your marriage mature.

FROM GOD'S WORD

Carry each other's burdens, and in this way you will fulfill the law of Christ. If anyone thinks he is something when he is nothing, he deceives himself. Each one should test his own actions. Then he can take pride in himself, without comparing himself to somebody else, for each one should carry his own load.

GALATIANS 6:2–5

REAL-LIFE SOUL MATES

We call ourselves the World's Most Opposite Couple, and we haven't found anyone yet who can top our list of differences. Even our spiritual gifts are different. Barb is a teacher. I am an exhorter. She wants to set a scriptural foundation before getting to the practical. I want to go right out and see if I can be slow to anger or love any enemy, but I sometimes go ahead of the Lord because I haven't gotten the big picture Barb has.

Because we are so different, attaining a spiritual oneness has not been easy. We went through some very hard times as we tried to fit together as "one flesh" like God wanted.

What we do have in common is the same heart and passion for the Lord and doing his work. We have the same goals for our ministries, even the ones we do separately, like Barb teaching a women's Bible study and me doing marriage counseling. God still speaks to us as a marriage team.

One of the things that has kept us unified is talking to audiences about marriage; we always teach side by side, giving them a complete picture of who we are as a couple.

One of our favorite spiritual times is going to dinner together. That's where we do our best sharing and communicating. We laugh and sometimes cry and sometimes share Scripture, but not always. Spiritual intimacy is not an event with us. It is an umbrella over all our interaction together.

CHUCK AND BARB SNYDER

❧ Your Turn

- The Bible emphasizes personal responsibility and free will. Why do you think this is part of the Gospel message?
- Have you noticed society's temptation to be a victim? Why do you think so many people are quick to blame others?
- Give an example of a time when you decided to rise above your negative circumstances. How did you adjust to something that was beyond your control? What allowed you to have a positive attitude?
- How does your partner demonstrate personal responsibility? What mature choices have you seen him or her make?
- In practical terms, what can you and your partner do to foster a blame-free relationship?

❧ Soul to Soul

To deepen your spiritual intimacy this next week, make note of:

- What you gained from this session together.
- A pressure point in your partner's upcoming week you will pray about.
- A concrete kindness you can offer your partner this week.

❧ Prayer

Dear God, help us to stay on the sidelines when others are playing the blame game. We strive to be responsible, to be accountable, and to be honest. Since these goals are hard to achieve consistently, we need your special help this week and in the weeks to come. Amen.

SESSION THIRTY-THREE:
YOU'RE NOT THE BOSS OF ME!

Chaim Potok's novel *The Chosen* tells the story of a young boy born to a Hasidic rabbi. As the boy matures, his father recognizes that his child is especially clever and gifted, if not already a little arrogant and impatient. Knowing that his boy was likely to become the rabbi of his people, the father makes a mysterious and difficult decision not to speak to the boy. He raised the boy in a house without the comfort of a speaking relationship. As the story draws to a close, Potok reveals that the father has chosen this unconventional path of parenthood with the boy because he wanted to create in him the capacity for understanding and compassion. He wanted him to minister from a heart that knows pain and can feel the pain of others. The father feared that his son's analytic brilliance and arrogance would rob him of the capacity to love.

The father in Potok's novel intuitively understood how keen, analytic abilities, unsoftened by emotional tenderness, lead to manipulation rather than ministry, how they lead to control rather than compassion.

You may not agree with this rabbi's methods, but it is difficult to dispute his insight. When your head is not linked to your heart, real love is difficult to muster—especially in marriage. The result is a spouse we sometimes call "The Controller."

Controllers, analytic by nature, typically use two powerful tools in gaining and maintaining control in their marriage. The first is fear. Controllers have refined the technique of "winning through intimidation." They have a hawklike eye for their partner's weakness, and their partner knows it. Without so much as a peep, the Controller can fire fear and anxiety into his or her mate like Rambo fires a machine gun.

The second tool of control is guilt. A Controlling husband can make his wife feel guilty for not having supper on the table at exactly 6:00. A Controlling wife can maneuver her husband into performing tasks for which she is actually responsible by laying on a sense of obligation and guilt. Controllers needle the conscience of their partner to provoke them to do what they want done.

The disciple Peter, in his own bungling way, was a Controller. He kept trying to tell Jesus what to do and what to say, to the point where Jesus rebuked him sharply: "Get behind me, Satan! You are a stumbling block to me; you do not have in mind the things of God, but the things of men" (Matt. 16:23). Finally, humbled by his denial of Jesus, Peter became an effective leader of the new church, even admitting his fault when Paul confronted him for forcing Gentiles to follow Jewish laws (Gal. 2:11–14).

Well, maybe you are lucky. Perhaps neither of you has controlling tendencies, but I (Les) do. I'm sometimes bossy with Leslie and feel compelled to give her unnecessary advice. Over the years, however, I've gotten better. Like Peter, I am willing to admit my faults. How about you?

From God's Word

You, then, why do you judge your brother? Or why do you look down on your brother? For we will all stand before God's judgment seat. It is written:

"'As surely as I live,' says the Lord,
'Every knee will bow before me;
every tongue will confess to God.'"

*So then, each of us will give an account of himself to God.
Therefore let us stop passing judgment on one another. Instead,
make up your mind not to put any stumbling block or obstacle in your
brother's way.*

ROMANS 14:10–13 ❧

❧ Your Turn

- How can you work together to keep the destructive influence of guilt and fear from entering into your marriage?
- Give an example of a time when you received compassion and understanding from your partner.
- Why do you think Christ so strongly admonishes us not to pass judgment on each other?
- Give an example of how you have been motivated to do something for your mate because you felt guilty?
- What is one step you can take together as a couple that will decrease controlling maneuvers in your relationship?

❧ Soul to Soul

To deepen your spiritual intimacy this next week, make note of:

- What you gained from this session together.
- A pressure point in your partner's upcoming week you will pray about.
- A concrete kindness you can offer your partner this week.

REAL-LIFE SOUL MATES

Although God ultimately holds the husband account-able for the leadership in the home, we strongly believe that marriage is a partnership between two equal participants. We believe the biblical truth that we are to become one (Genesis 2:24), and we try to model this in our relationship. It has not been easy. God intended marriage to be the clos-est human bond. All too often, however, the stressors that invade a marriage pull spouses apart. We suggest three things you can do to build and strengthen your partnership and help protect it from these pressures.

First, surrender your marriage to God. To grow together, you and your spouse must yield yourselves fully to the Lord. This involves taking time to pray and discuss the Scriptures together regularly, if not daily. Graciously, lov-ingly, encourage your mate to take an active role in your spiritual partnership. God understands you and your mate perfectly and can empower you with his Holy Spirit to build your spiritual relationship.

Second, agree to walk together. Early in our relation-ship Vonette and I agreed that our partnership would not be my way or Vonette's way but our way—serving the Lord together.

Finally, protect your relationship by sharing each other's dreams. Vonette and I have had many dreams through the years, but the single most important objective of our lives is to help fulfill the Great Commission of our Lord, as described in Matthew 28:19–20. These are our expressions of our love for the Lord, our deep gratitude for all that he has done for us, and our desire to obey him.

BILL AND VONETTE BRIGHT

❧ Prayer

Dear God, we long for a love that is free from fear and guilt. Help us to work on relinquishing our controlling tendencies and exchange them for genuine love that works in the situations of our lives. May we feel the pain but multiply the joys of each other as our marriage moves forward for another week. Amen.

SESSION THIRTY-FOUR:
SEX, SEX, SEX . . .
ENOUGH ALREADY!

In the film *Annie Hall*, Woody Allen and Diane Keaton are shown split-screen as each talks to an analyst about their sexual relationship. When the analyst asks how often they have sex, he answers, "Hardly ever, maybe three times a week," while she describes it as, "Constantly, three times a week."

How is it that a husband and wife can view sex so differently? One reason is that they are socialized in different ways about sexuality and marriage. Men tend to see sex as a pleasurable, physical activity, while women see it as a sign of emotional commitment. These separate meanings can become the source of much miscommunication and misunderstanding in marriage. Consider the following comments made by a wife and husband after three or four years of marriage:

> Wife: He keeps saying he wants to make love, but it doesn't feel like love to me. Sometimes I feel bad that I feel that way, but I just can't help it.
> Husband: I don't understand. She says it doesn't feel like love. What does that mean, anyway? What does she think love is? I want to have sex with her because I love her!

In this marriage, as in many others, the husband sees himself as showing his love to his wife by engaging her in sexual activity. The wife, on the other hand, sees sexual activity as something that should evolve out of verbal expressions of affection and love. Like a scene from a Woody Allen movie that cuts too close to home, this couple bickers continually about how frequently they have sex.

Of course, the question about how much lovemaking is enough is not a matter of counting the number of times per week that a Christian couple may decently have sex. There is no prescription, no magic number. For partners who are dedicated to the personal life of each other, the question of frequency will be answered in terms of concern for the needs and desires of the other person.

Our friend and former professor, Lewis Smedes, says this in his book *Sex for Christians*: "The moral issue is never 'how much' sex but whether physical sex is being integrated into a pattern of personal dedication. What happens 'between the times' is more important than how many times."

Spouses need to be realistic about their sex life and willing to accommodate each other's desires. Granted, not every sexual experience is going to be equally satisfying and fulfilling for both partners. But if you rejoice in the husband or wife of your youth, you will be captivated by each other's love (see Prov. 5:18–20).

FROM GOD'S WORD

I belong to my lover, and his desire is for me. Come, my lover, let us go to the countryside, let us spend the night in the villages. Let us go early to the vineyards to see if the vines have budded, if their blossoms have opened, and if the pomegranates are in bloom—there I will give you my love.

SONG OF SONGS 7:10–12 ❧

❧ **Your Turn**

- Do you identify with the scenario in the opening paragraph of this session? Why or why not?

REAL-LIFE SOUL MATES

We cultivate spiritual intimacy in our marriage through the traditional means—praying together, participating in a weekly Bible study with other couples, and enjoying Communion every Sunday. But more and more we are finding that the time we spend before falling asleep, when we snuggle close and share intimate conversation, is some of the most precious. Especially in our playful lovemaking, Christ's kingdom is brought into our hearts and into our marriage in a unique way. In lovemaking we become delightfully abandoned and vulnerably trusting. Excitement and an overwhelming sense of oneness invade our lives as we mutually nurture and frolic with curiosity and awe—all very spiritual concepts as God teaches us marvelous lessons about celebration and pleasure.

Meaningful touch often nurtures the deeper spiritual parts of our being. Colossians 3:12–14 tells us to cultivate gentleness, kindness, humility, empathy, forgiveness, and, above all, love. In a marvelous manner, our lovemaking helps us bring these qualities into our marriage and has brought us closer to our Creator and to the spiritual one-flesh partnership he desires. Thank you, Lord!

DOUG AND CATHERINE ROSENAU

- What causes tension in your sexual relations? What, if anything, do you conflict about and why?
- Give an example of an intimate encounter with your partner that brought you deep emotional fulfillment. What made it that way for you?
- Discuss how your sexuality can be woven into a pattern of personal dedication as a couple. What concrete steps can each of you take toward this goal?
- How can you infuse your sexual intimacy with more physical pleasure?

﷼ Soul to Soul

To deepen your spiritual intimacy this next week, make note of:

- What you gained from this session together.
- A pressure point in your partner's upcoming week you will pray about.
- A concrete kindness you can offer your partner this week.

﷼ Prayer

Almighty God, allow us to experience the fullness of rejoicing in each other's love. Uphold us as we seek to weave sexual intimacy into a pattern of personal dedication to one another. Help us as a couple to satisfy the desires of our hearts. In the name of Christ, amen.

SESSION THIRTY-FIVE:
PAY NOW, PLAY LATER

We have always had separate closets. And it's a good thing. Mine is a total wreck. Les's closet, however, looks like a page from *Architectural Digest*. He has a place for everything and takes the time to put things where they belong. I, on the other hand, put things wherever it is convenient ... the back of a chair, the floor. You get the picture.

Well, Les has never been too pushy as a neat-nic, but his self-discipline has rubbed off. Not that my clothes routinely make it onto cedar hangers, but I have come to appreciate a particular quality of the highly organized—*delayed gratification*. It's the ability to patiently put off immediate rewards in order to enjoy greater benefits later on.

Saving money is a prime example. Two years into our marriage, the only vehicle we had, a gray Ford pickup truck, was on its last legs. "Yippee!" I thought to myself. I was ready to cruise the car lots and bring home a new sporty model. "We could probably get a new car for $300 a month," I told Les.

He had another idea: "Don't you think we'd be better off to avoid the interest of a loan and pay cash for a car?" The thought had never occurred to me. But we began to talk about how we could cut back on this and that, and we soon came up with a plan to delay our immediate desires and enjoy the freedom of a new car debt-free. We have paid cash for every car we've had since.

But delayed gratification does not just apply to saving money. It is a principle that applies to living. Scott Peck, in his best-selling book *The Road Less Traveled*, states: "Delaying gratification is a process of scheduling the pain and pleasure of life in such a way as to enhance the pleasure by meeting and experiencing the pain first and getting it over with. It is the only decent way to live." Scheduling the easy and the hard applies to everything from cleaning the house to earning an education.

The key to delayed gratification is patience. It's a virtue endorsed by Scripture. Patience, for example, is a fruit of the Spirit (Gal. 5:22). As Paul prayed for Christians he often asked God to give them patience (Col. 1:11). Timothy was commended by Paul for his patience (2 Tim. 3:10). And the book of Hebrews characterizes the Christian life as an exercise in patience (12:1–3). But the ultimate example of delayed gratification and patience is Christ (see 2 Peter 3:9, 15). When the devil tempted him with the splendor of "all the kingdoms of the world," Jesus refused, knowing that he would ultimately enter the kingdom of God (Matt. 4:1–11).

Putting our immediate gratification temporarily in abeyance can strengthen the marriage bond. Couples who do not develop the capacity for delayed gratification become impulsive and are soon swayed by every whim of the moment. But couples who forgo some instant pleasures to cultivate the discipline of delaying their gratification reap meaningful and fulfilling rewards. "Patience," as a German proverb says, "is a bitter plant, but it bears sweet fruit."

FROM GOD'S WORD

Therefore, since we are surrounded by such a great cloud of witnesses, let us throw off everything that hinders and the sin that so easily entangles, and let us run with perseverance the race marked out for us. Let us fix our eyes on Jesus, the author and perfecter of our faith, who for the joy set before him endured the cross, scorning its shame, and sat down at the right hand of the throne of God. Consider him who endured such opposition from sinful men, so that you will not grow weary and lose heart.

HEBREWS 12:1–3 ❧

REAL-LIFE SOUL MATES

We started our marriage as two individuals in love but traveling parallel paths. Over thirty-seven years of marriage we have watched God bring these paths together as one. We were always committed to one another, but the total oneness of heart and soul grew gradually.

What caused our paths to join rather than diverge? The joining was based on our deep commitment to God and to one another. Busy schedules, work, and the demands of growing children tested these commitments, and we opted for an intense array of external activities and spiritual outreach to the neglect of developing our own relationship. Finally, the strain got our attention and we began to develop a deeper interaction with each other. As a result, our bond grew strong: We learned to give each other space, to laugh at ourselves, and to encourage each other's goals. We renewed our common vision for evangelism and discipleship, and we devoted our home and time to that end. In our critical life decisions we made sure that we both had clear direction from God.

More importantly, we have found that sorrows and troubles have deepened our soul relationship much more than times of accomplishment and success. Our son's death at age thirty drew us together powerfully. We continue to learn tolerance and appreciation for one another because we are not the same people who married thirty-seven years ago: We are soul mates changing and growing together.

JERRY AND MARY WHITE

❧ Your Turn

- Discuss how each of you practices the art of delaying your gratification. Does it come easier to one of you than it does the other?
- Give an example of how you personally have patiently practiced delayed gratification.
- How do patience and delayed gratification relate to your spiritual journey with Christ?
- Name one or two areas in your lives that could benefit from the discipline of delayed gratification. How could you as a couple practice it?
- How could practicing delayed gratification buoy your marriage?

❧ Soul to Soul

To deepen your spiritual intimacy this next week, make note of:

- What you gained from this session together.
- A pressure point in your partner's upcoming week you will pray about.
- A concrete kindness you can offer your partner this week.

❧ Prayer

Gracious God, we thank you for patience, one of the fruits of your Spirit. Help us to encourage its growth and development in our marriage. We want to make choices based on wisdom instead of ease. Reveal to us the rewards that come in delaying our gratification for better results. Amen.

❧

SESSION THIRTY-SIX:
HOW TO BE A WISE GUY (AND GAL)

Falling in love is a dizzying experience. Once the spark of attraction catches flame, love quickly turns into a raging fire of unreasoned passion. Engulfed by its heat, couples sometimes sacrifice all sound judgment in the interest of bonding their relationship. The Song of Songs says, "Many waters cannot quench love; rivers cannot wash it away" (8:7). Love, by its very nature, is extravagant.

We read recently about a man who hired a helicopter to drop 2,500 carnations and 10,000 love letters on the lawn of a woman he loved. Apparently the woman failed to share this man's affection and had him charged with littering. She told reporters "he had lost his mind."

Love really can cause some people to lose their heads. They become "crazy in love." They become compelled by the emotional force of love and forsake their analytical ability. It's a common danger. The compelling emotional force overrides our capacity to think clearly if we let it. That is why Scripture urges us to "be careful, then, how you live—not as unwise, but as wise" (Eph. 5:15).

Have you thought much about wisdom—the ability to reason with insight? You should. It is essential to the success of your marriage. Sure, the emotional side of love is vital, and you will need to stoke the fires of passion over the years, but don't neglect the cool calm of wisdom.

Wisdom is not about saying wise words or doing wise deeds. It is concerned with *being*, not *doing*. So how do you cultivate wisdom in marriage? Or, as Job asked, "Where can wisdom be found? Where does understanding dwell?" (28:12). The writer of Proverbs compared searching for wisdom to mining and said, "If you look for it as for silver and search for it as for hidden treasure, then you will understand" (2:4–5).

After a decade of marriage we are still on an expedition for more wisdom. Daily we seek to avoid being unwise and we have discovered two tools that are essential in our pursuit.

First of all, we have learned that wisdom only comes when we are humble. As Socrates said, "The wisest man is he who knows his own ignorance." Without humility marriage partners fall victim to pride, and "when pride comes, then comes disgrace, but with humility comes wisdom" (Prov. 11:2). So be humble enough to ask for help. Learn how to ask a good question. According to Francis Bacon, "A prudent question is one-half of wisdom."

The second tool for mining wisdom in marriage stems from the first—ask God to share his wisdom with you (see James 1:5). Human wisdom on its own is inadequate (see 1 Cor. 1:19; 1:21; 3:18–19). We need the wisdom that comes from God, for "the fear of the LORD is the beginning of wisdom" (Ps. 111:10; see also Prov. 9:10; Matt. 12:42; 13:54; Acts 6:3).

So enjoy the dizzying emotions of love when they come, but never neglect the importance of wisdom in marriage. It is a shared pursuit for soul mates and it will bless your union.

FROM GOD'S WORD

Blessed is the man who finds wisdom, the man who gains understanding, for she is more profitable than silver and yields better returns than gold. She is more precious than rubies; nothing you desire can compare with her. Long life is in her right hand; in her left hand are riches and honor. Her ways are pleasant ways, and all her paths are peace. She is a tree of life to those who embrace her; those who lay hold of her will be blessed.

PROVERBS 3:13–18 ❧

❧ Your Turn

- Scripture points to the fact that wisdom is more about who you are as a person than it is about what you say or do. What do you make of this?
- Was there a time in your relationship when the emotions of love overruled sound judgment? What can you learn from that experience?
- Give an example of a time when you humbled yourself to ask for help. How did it increase your wisdom?
- Is it a struggle for you to ask for help? How about your partner? Does it prevent either one of you from becoming "wise"?
- In what areas do you find that your spouse is especially wise? How did he or she develop that wisdom?

❧ Soul to Soul

To deepen your spiritual intimacy this next week, make note of:

- What you gained from this session together.
- A pressure point in your partner's upcoming week you will pray about.
- A concrete kindness you can offer your partner this week.

REAL-LIFE SOUL MATES

In over thirty-five years of marriage one of the discoveries that Joyce and I have made is this: Developing our spiritual intimacy is the foundation for a lasting marriage. And it is more than doing activities together; it's an attitude or an atmosphere within the marriage relationship. It's the feeling of freedom that you can connect at any time and in any way about spiritual matters or issues. There is no walking on eggshells about sharing or raising a question. You live your lives in the confidence that you are connected spiritually.

In terms of the specifics of our spiritual growth together, we each maintain our own personal devotional life. This involves daily prayer with a specific list of prayer requests. We read from both the Old and New Testaments as well as devotional reading. Some days we read separate material, but on others it is the same. Our together times consist of one of us praying aloud fairly regularly. Often during the day we will bring to the other's attention a prayer request. Much of the time we read a devotional aloud and have used several. Our worshiping together at church is very important to us, and frequently we talk about our response to the music or message as we drive home.

Perhaps sharing the mutual grief over the life and death of our retarded son during the past twenty-seven years was a factor that brought us together spiritually. Through this we learned to share our hurts, concerns, frustrations, and joys together. What has ministered to us both at these times was worship—not only at church, but at home through worship music from a multitude of Christian artists and numerous music and inspirational videos. We have found that our personal and corporate walk with the Lord must be a priority and a commitment just as much as our wedding vows.

H. NORMAN AND JOYCE WRIGHT

❧ Prayer

Gracious God, you have promised to give wisdom generously to all who ask. And now we are asking. Fill us with wisdom as we invest our time, talents, and resources in our shared future. Build us up into people of humility who are quick to learn and quick to seek your counsel. Amen.

Session Thirty-Seven:
The Role of Optimism in Marriage

Ron and Cindy came to us after three years of marriage, because they were calling it quits. We were their last-ditch effort to save a sinking marriage. Soon into our first counseling session we saw just why this young couple was already throwing in the towel. They were pessimists, defeated, disappointed, and depressed. They never expected their marriage to get any better. All they could see were problems, no solutions. So they gave up hope.

Nothing is more deadly to marriage than negativism, especially in its most alluring form of pessimism. In fact, if couples could be given a vaccine against pessimistic thinking we would see the divorce rate all but drop off. In a sense, you can protect your marriage against a pessimistic virus. All it takes is a good shot of optimism.

No psychologist has helped us understand optimism more than Dr. Martin Seligman at the University of Pennsylvania. As a twenty-one-year-old graduate student fresh out of college, he observed an experiment that sent him on a lifelong quest to find out why some people seek opportunity while others give up.

In the experiment Dr. Seligman observed, dogs were subjected to a minor shock, which they could avoid by jumping over a low wall separating two sides of a shuttle box. Most dogs learned this task easily. But other dogs just lay down whimpering. They had no will to try. When Seligman investigated the dogs who had given up, he found they had been used in a prior experiment in which they received shocks no matter what they did. These dogs had "learned" helplessness. Because they had been given shocks regardless of whether they struggled or jumped or barked or did nothing, they learned that nothing they did mattered. So why try?

Like Seligman's dogs, marriages can fall victim to learned helplessness. When a couple begins to see every problem as interminable, or when they believe one problem will ruin everything, they quit trying. They raise the white flag and surrender to problems they could otherwise beat. *You and I are never going to be any different*, they reason, *so why try?*

Someone defined a pessimist as one who feels bad when he feels good for fear he'll feel worse when he feels better. Pessimists have simply made negative thinking a habit, a way of life. Optimists, on the other hand, are undaunted by defeat. When they are confronted with the inevitable hard knocks of life, they immediately look for solutions. They see defeat as temporary.

The Bible has a different word for optimism—*hope*. In the New Testament, the word "hope" appears more than eighty times, and it usually refers to Christ, who is the hope of this world (see Titus 2:13; 1 Peter 1:3). Colossians 1:5 tells us that love springs from hope. Another New Testament writer called hope "an anchor for the soul, firm and secure" (Heb. 6:19), and Paul said it "does not disappoint us" (Rom. 5:5). He also alluded to hope as being an attitude of optimism when he urged the Thessalonians to put on "hope . . . as a helmet" (1 Thess. 5:8). Hope protects our head. It is an attitude that safeguards optimism and protects a marriage.

FROM GOD'S WORD

For in this hope we were saved. But hope that is seen is no hope at all. Who hopes for what he already has? But if we hope for what we do not yet have, we wait for it patiently.

ROMANS 8:24–25 ❧

REAL-LIFE SOUL MATES

Philippians 1:6 says that you can have confidence that since God began a good work in you he will bring it to completion. Since becoming soul mates is his desire, you can rest in that confidence.

As I looked back at our own experience I realized that there were a few keys to becoming closer spiritually: acceptance, humility, and communication, each making the next possible. Together these ingredients move the relationship toward the oneness we yearned for. Louis and I become closest when we move past our individual pride and become vulnerable. When we feel accepted rather than judged, vulnerability is safer to risk. When I sense him being vulnerable I feel very tender toward him. Spiritual intimacy is inextricably wrapped up with all the other aspects of your marriage. Becoming soul mates can enhance "being best friends," finding sexual enjoyment, and attaining the emotional fulfillment that marriage was designed to achieve.

We no longer have to compare our degree of spiritual oneness with anything other than the closeness with the Lord that we each want for ourselves. So sharing our deepest spiritual concern or expressing our gratitude for God's goodness to us brings a higher level of oneness.

LOUIS AND MELISSA MCBURNEY

❧ Your Turn

- Why do you think hope is talked about so often in Scripture?
- Give an example of a time when you saw your partner demonstrate hope and optimism.
- Have you ever fallen victim of learned helplessness and given up hope? What did you do to overcome it?
- Talk about the home you grew up in. Was it basically optimistic or pessimistic? What can each of you learn about being optimists from your families?
- Is there something right now in your life that could be given a boost with a shot of optimism? How can you help each other cultivate this virtue?

❧ Soul to Soul

To deepen your spiritual intimacy this next week, make note of:

- What you gained from this session together.
- A pressure point in your partner's upcoming week you will pray about.
- A concrete kindness you can offer your partner this week.

❧ Prayer

To you, O Lord, we lift up our souls because we trust in you. We proclaim confidently that our hope is in you. In the midst of our discouragements help us to take refuge, together, in our ultimate Hope. Infuse our marriage relationship with a continuing attitude of optimism. Amen.

SESSION THIRTY-EIGHT:

THE VALUE OF TENDER TOUCH

In May 1985, Brigitte Gerney was trapped for six hours beneath a thirty-five-ton collapsed construction crane in New York City. Throughout her ordeal, she held the hand of officer Paul Ragonese, who stayed by her side as heavy machinery moved the tons of twisted steel from her crushed legs. A stranger's touch gave her hope and the will to live.

Touch is one of the most powerful communication tools. From a mother's cradling embrace to a friend's comforting hug or a marriage partner's caress, touch has the special power to send messages of union and communion. Even a momentary and seemingly incidental touch on your partner's shoulder or hand can strengthen the marital bond by conveying affirmation, comfort, and security.

Both the toucher and the one being touched receive emotional and physiological benefits. Stacks of research, for example, have shown that a gentle touch or hug can cause a speeding heart to quiet, soaring blood pressure to drop, and severe pain to ease. A study at UCLA estimated that if some "type-A driven" men would hug their wives several times each day, it would increase their life span by almost two years, not to mention the way it would improve their marriages. That same study reported that eight to ten meaningful touches each day help us maintain emotional and physical health.

Scripture shows the value of touch as it conveys a blessing (see Gen. 27:26; Gen. 48:9–14). In the Old Testament, the people laid their hands on the Levites to demonstrate that they were setting them apart for their priestly duties (Num. 8:10). Moses laid his hands on Joshua to symbolize that he was giving Joshua authority over the people (Num. 27:18). And Jesus, of course, was a master of communicating love through touch: "And he took the children in his arms, put his hands on them and blessed them" (Mark 10:16).

So consider the value of meaningful touch to your marriage. If a stranger's touch meant life to Brigitte Gerney, think of what a meaningful touch from you can do for your partner.

FROM GOD'S WORD

Just then a woman who had been subject to bleeding for twelve years came up behind him and touched the edge of his cloak. She said to herself, "If I only touch his cloak, I will be healed."

Jesus turned and saw her. "Take heart, daughter," he said, "your faith has healed you." And the woman was healed from that moment.

MATTHEW 9:20–22 ᛩ

Filled with compassion, Jesus reached out his hand and touched the man. . . . Immediately the leprosy left him and he was cured.

MARK 1:41–42 ᛩ

ᛩ Your Turn

- Why do you think Christ was so attuned to personal touch?
- Give an example of how you benefited from a recent touch from your partner.
- When do you most often want to be touched by your partner and in what ways?

REAL-LIFE SOUL MATES

When Shirley and I were married at age nineteen in Nashville, Mack Craig gave us a Bible with our married names on it. It's the only wedding gift that has stayed with us through the years. We've read it together, we've prayed together, and we've always been faithful in church attendance and activity.

And still we almost "came unglued."

The entertainment business takes a terrible toll on marriages. The stress and temptations tore at the very under-pinnings of our marriage, and for two years we thought it was over. But one day, walking past the piano in our living room, I focused on a picture of Shirley that I'd seen count-less times before. This time it transfixed me. It was a picture of her at the age of three, with her arms around her father, Red Foley, and the adoring, needful, poignant expression of that little girl seared itself into my heart. I realized that she was still that little girl. Oh, she was now in her thirties with four kids, and a wonderful wife and mother. I was used to seeing her as a grown woman, with some of the wounds and resulting defenses right at the surface. Her dad had recently gone to be with the Lord, and I knew that little girl still needed a man to protect, love, and nurture her.

Suddenly, I wanted to be that man. I shared that with her, and we shared some tears. The next Father's Day, she gave me a framed picture of her as a little girl, and on the back she wrote: "Take care of this little girl—she needs you."

It's been twenty-five years or more now, and I pray and worship with that little girl, my grown-up wife, all the time. We're growing older, but we're still kids to each other—and somehow, kids can just love God and each other better than grown-ups. What was it that Jesus said? "Except you become like little children, you shall in no wise enter into the King-dom of Heaven" (Matthew 18:2).

PAT AND SHIRLEY BOONE

- Do you feel differently about touching in public and in private?
- What is the one thing you would like your partner to understand about you and touching?

Soul to Soul

To deepen your spiritual intimacy this next week, make note of:

- What you gained from this session together.
- A pressure point in your partner's upcoming week you will pray about.
- A concrete kindness you can offer your partner this week.

Prayer

Gracious God, we thank you for the meaning—even the healing—of one human being reaching out to touch another person. Your touch gives us hope and motivation to reach out our healing arms to one another. We thank you for the precious gift of a gentle caress. Help us to practice the ministry of meaningful touch with each other this week. Amen.

SESSION THIRTY-NINE:

NO ONE NEEDS
TO BE A FOOL

A young bride, getting settled into the routine of married life, cooked a ham for her new husband. Before putting it in the pan, she cut off both ends. When her husband asked her why she did that, she replied that her mother had always done it that way. At a later date, when they were having a baked ham dinner at her mother's home, the young husband asked his mother-in-law, casually, why she cut both ends of the ham. The mother shrugged and said she really didn't know, except that her mother had always done it that way. Finally, he asked the grandmother why she always cut the ends off the ham before she baked it. The grandmother looked at him suspiciously, replying, "Because my baking dish was too small!"

Sometimes, without even knowing it, we do silly things. And while needlessly baking a sawed off ham has no serious effects, some blunders can lead to downright foolish results. Is *foolish* too strong a word? Probably not. "A fool," said William Thackeray, "can no more see his own folly than he can see his ears."

We know a couple, married six years, who didn't make it. They made some foolish choices and never had a clue as to how they were blowing their marriage apart. Everything started out fine. In fact it was more than fine. They came from good homes and were raised in the church. They had more advantages for a successful marriage than most. But somewhere along the line they began to take their heritage and their relationship with God for granted. Slowly, they gravitated away from their values and made compromises with their faith. His business involved traveling and their frequent separations became ripe for foolish decisions. It was then only a matter of time before the relationship folded.

We can never totally escape silly blunders; that's what makes life interesting. But no one needs to be a fool. For according to Scripture there is really only one thing that can make anyone a fool—missing out on God's will. Paul says, "Do not be foolish, but understand what the Lord's will is" (Eph. 5:17).

Every couple needs the wisdom that comes in seeking God's will for their relationship. Without God's direction, foolish decisions are bound to happen and then a string of side effects appear. The Bible says that a fool is quick to quarrel (Prov. 20:3), scorns wisdom (Prov. 23:9), repeats mistakes again and again (Prov. 26:11), has no peace (Prov. 29:9), can't control his anger (Prov. 29:11), and is cocky (Prov. 30:32). Can you imagine trying to live with the person who is not seeking the Lord's will? "Better to meet a bear robbed of her cubs," says Proverbs, "than a fool in his folly" (17:12).

From God's Word

Be very careful, then, how you live—not as unwise but as wise, making the most of every opportunity, because the days are evil. Therefore do not be foolish, but understand what the Lord's will is. Do not get drunk on wine, which leads to debauchery. Instead, be filled with the Spirit.
                                    Ephesians 5:15–18 ❧

❧ Your Turn

- How have you sought God's will in your life and what difference has it made?
- Wise decisions take time. What goes into your decision making process as a couple?

Real-Life Soul Mates

Spiritual intimacy. The very words hang heavy with an aura of the ethereal, unattainable, and unreachable.

Early in our marriage we decided we weren't going to "program" spiritual intimacy into our lives, thus setting ourselves up for failure. Because of work, school, and small children, the set-time spiritual schedule was more of a burden than a blessing.

Instead, we chose to view spiritual intimacy as a natural, spontaneous, and foundational means of relating to each other. Spiritual intimacy is not something we do: It literally defines who we are as a couple. However, we have made some intentional decisions to develop our spiritual relationship. We make a conscious effort to share some spiritual question as it relates to a family problem, a book we've been reading, a sermon in the making, a Bible study lesson, or even political issues. The discussions may take place on the phone, over a meal, walking, riding in the car, in bed, or even in the church foyer between services. The point is, not a day passes when we don't connect as a couple with the bigger spiritual picture of life.

The days have now stretched into twenty-three years of marriage. Spiritual intimacy is as attainable, practical, and natural to us as developing a family budget.

We can think of no greater marital legacy than to be known as spiritual intimates.

Gary and Jorie Gulbranson

- Many things can lead to foolish choices. Chief among them is anger. Has anger ever led you to a foolish choice? How?
- If you were to be as specific as possible, what do you think God's will for your marriage is this week?
- In practical terms, what can you and your partner do to protect your marriage against foolish choices?

❧ Soul to Soul

To deepen your spiritual intimacy this next week, make note of:
- What you gained from this session together.
- A pressure point in your partner's upcoming week you will pray about.
- A concrete kindness you can offer your partner this week.

❧ Prayer

Almighty God, we recognize the need for good judgment in all we do. Save us from the misjudgments that come in being hasty or superficial. Teach us to depend on the wisdom of people we trust. And most of all, teach us to hear your still, small voice which is so easily drowned out by the racket of everyday living. Amen.

Session Forty:

Having
the Tithe of Your Life

Religious reformer Martin Luther observed, "There are three conversions necessary: the conversion of the heart, mind, and the purse." Of the three, the purse can be the most difficult for some. Especially in marriage. Agreeing on money matters is always an emotional proposition, and for many couples, tithes and offerings present a special challenge.

A fundamental shift of attitude toward giving took place in our home when we changed the question we were asking of each other. Rather than, "How much of our money should we give to God?" we learned to ask, "How much of God's money should we spend on ourselves?" The difference between these two questions was monumental for us. It helped us to remember that our financial resources are not part ours and part God's. Our income is *all* God's (see Job 41:11; Exod. 19:5–6; Ps. 24:1). With this understanding as a starting point, we eliminated much of the legalistic thinking and guilt related to giving based on a set percentage of income. John Wesley understood this when he said, "Gain all you can, save all you can, give all you can."

Another principle that has helped us comes from 2 Corinthians 8, where we are told how the Macedonians gave. Paul writes: "For I testify that they gave as much as they were able, and even beyond their ability. Entirely on their own, they urgently pleaded with us for the privilege of sharing in this service to the saints" (8:3–4). They gave voluntarily, not because somebody twisted their arms behind their backs. They *wanted* to share in the joy of helping. A little later in that same letter, the apostle encourages this spirit of voluntary spontaneity in giving: "Each man should give what he has decided in his heart to give, not reluctantly or under compulsion, for God loves a cheerful giver" (9:7).

Why is our motivation in giving so important? Well, consider the Pharisees and teachers of the law who used tithing to camouflage their selfishness. They were so ritualistic about tithing that they would count the small herbs in their garden to be sure they were tithing on all they had. Of course, they were missing the whole point. Listen to what Jesus said to them: "Woe to you, teachers of the law and Pharisees, you hypocrites! You give a tenth of your spices—mint, dill and cummin. But you have neglected the more important matters of the law—justice, mercy and faithfulness. You should have practiced the latter, without neglecting the former. You blind guides! You strain out a gnat but swallow a camel" (Matt. 23:23–24).

The point of tithing, of giving a portion of your income to support the ministry of the church, is not to keep a legalistic check-list and to compulsively count out "God's part." The point is that we are simply stewards of all he has given us. And by giving a portion of what he has given us, we become converted *from* money and converted *to* him.

Here's the bottom line. The Bible calls us to "profane" the god of money by giving it away. And to do that, we must take Christ's famous exhortation and apply it to our checkbooks: "Where your treasure is," Jesus said, "there your heart will be also" (Matt. 6:21).

FROM GOD'S WORD

We—the priests, the Levites and the people—have cast lots to determine when each of our families is to bring to the house of our God at set times each year a contribution of wood to burn on the altar

179

of the LORD our God, as it is written in the Law. We also assume responsibility for bringing to the house of the LORD each year the first-fruits of our crops and of every fruit tree.

NEHEMIAH 10:34–35 ❧

❧ Your Turn

- Jesus counsels us not to "store up treasures on earth." How do you understand and live out this concept?
- Give an example of a time when you identified a financial need and gave as a team to help meet that need.
- What struggles have you encountered in trying to agree on joint giving? What are you doing to resolve them?
- Take some time to conduct a financial inventory. Identify any changes you might make in the ways you spend and give money as a couple.
- In practical and specific terms, how can the two of you more effectively share in the joy of giving?

❧ Soul to Soul

To deepen your spiritual intimacy this next week, make note of:

- What you gained from this session together.
- A pressure point in your partner's upcoming week you will pray about.
- A concrete kindness you can offer your partner this week.

REAL-LIFE SOUL MATES

The way Elaine and I sustain spiritual intimacy is threefold: First, we genuinely experience conversations (prayer) together with God. Furthermore, we have ongoing discussions concerning biblical texts. Finally, we observe the "Christian" calendar. We deliberately nurture memories based upon the sacred seasons.

The way we celebrate sacred seasons can be seen in our keeping of Advent. Several years ago, we developed our own family tradition of gathering around the Advent wreath in our living room. We light the appropriate candles each evening, as we anticipate the coming of our Messiah King. This precious time consists of sharing memories, reading and discussing biblical texts, sharing hopes for tomorrow, and praying together.

Observing Advent allows us to anticipate the "breaking in" of God in our marriage, family, and world. It allows us to focus on the presence of God in our daily lives. Advent becomes a season that is not frantic with places to go and gifts to buy. This is just one example of how the keeping of the Christian calendar has transformed secular time into sacred moments that allow for spiritual intimacy.

STEVE AND ELAINE GREEN

❧ Prayer

Gracious God, we know you value generosity because you gave so much and you have promised to bless and refresh us when we give. You have even linked our kindness to those in need with the greatest honor of all: ministry to you, our Creator and King. Grant us a spirit of gladness in giving together and always make us generous. Amen.

SESSION FORTY-ONE:

AVOIDING THE NUMBER-ONE MARRIAGE PROBLEM

"You're not listening to me!"

We hear this statement more than any other when counseling couples. No surprise. The number-one marriage problem reported by couples is a breakdown of communication.

A sage once said that the Lord gave us two ears and one mouth, and that ratio ought to tell us something. Good point. We often think about "good communication skills" as learning to express ourselves more clearly, getting our message across. However, ninety-eight percent of good communication is listening.

Listening is not passive. It is not sitting back, quietly hearing what our partner has to say, waiting for our turn to talk. Listening is active. It is getting involved with your partner's message to accurately understand it. The point of active listening is to let your partner know you are in tune with him or her. That's all. A good listener doesn't give advice or try to solve problems with sermons and testimonies. A good listener listens.

Consider this typical interaction:

Wife: I don't know what to tell Melody. She wanted to ride with us to the game this weekend and I said okay, but then I remembered I had already invited Tim and Sarah.

Husband: Um-m.

Wife: So what should we do?

Husband: About what?

Wife: About Melody. There's not enough room for her to ride with us.

Husband: Well, then she can't ride with us. Just call her and tell her.

Wife: I know. I know. But . . . you don't understand.

Husband: I'm listening.

Is he really? We don't think so. He may be hearing his wife's words, but he is not understanding his wife's feelings. She is not wanting him to solve her problem as much as she is wanting him to understand how lousy she feels. If he were actively listening, he would have said something like, "Sounds like you are afraid of hurting Melody's feelings." That's all. No fix-it solutions. Simply identifying the real message is what listening is about.

Jesus understood the importance of listening. Even as a young boy he sat with the teachers in the temple, "listening to them and asking them questions [and] everyone . . . was amazed at his understanding" (Luke 2:46–47). The apostle Paul understood that listening requires diligent work. When he was before Agrippa, he said, "I beg you to listen to me patiently" (Acts 26:3). The book of James tells us to "be quick to listen, slow to speak" (James 1:19). And the book of Proverbs says, "He who answers before listening—that is his folly and his shame" (18:13).

The word *listen* occurs more than two hundred times in the Bible. It is a practice that is essential to all relationships and especially marriage. So the next time you are eager to quickly solve your partner's problems, make sure you first understand his or her feelings.

FROM GOD'S WORD

Surely the arm of the LORD is not too short to save, nor his ear too dull to hear. But your iniquities have separated you from your

God; your sins have hidden his face from you, so that he will not hear. For your hands are stained with blood, your fingers with guilt. Your lips have spoken lies, and your tongue mutters wicked things.

ISAIAH 59:1–3 ⪧

⪧ Your Turn

- Why do you think the Bible so often emphasizes the ability to listen? Why does it single it out as a mark of wisdom?
- What is one thing you would like your partner to understand about your need to be listened to and understood? How would you like him or her to improve as a listener?
- Give an example of how you benefited from a recent time of communication with your partner—a time when he or she was an especially good listener.
- When do you most often want to be listened to by your partner? How do you convey this to him or her? Or do you?
- Do you feel that gender differences help or complicate listening? Give examples to support your comments.

⪧ Soul to Soul

To deepen your spiritual intimacy this next week, make note of:

- What you gained from this session together.
- A pressure point in your partner's upcoming week you will pray about.
- A concrete kindness you can offer your partner this week.

REAL-LIFE SOUL MATES

There was something romantic about the fisherman's walk that passed our place on the rock ribbed coast of Maine.

The walk was there because a law in Maine required every property owner on the coast to provide a walkway for fishermen to use in recovering their lobster pots and other gear after a storm. These walkways stretched for miles and miles with new, inspiring vistas around every cove.

It was the privilege of people like Lora Lee and me to walk that shoreline. The spray enlivened our faces. The wind beat against our rubberized yellow parkas. On clear days, it seemed like we could almost see Europe. And we always felt drawn to God and to each other.

And here, hand in hand, for long, unhurried walks, our souls caught up and our spirits melded.

Sometimes we just stood looking east, absorbing the sea. At other times we talked about our future, our children, our problems, or even our fears.

We never declared it to be so, but the talk was always about us, never about the nation or the world. The fisherman's walk was the place we faced ourselves as reflected in each other. In its own way, this was a spiritual experience that brought us closer to God and to each other.

Later, when we moved from New England to the prairies of Illinois, we achieved the same results when she and I sat together in the cozy environment of moving shadows and green and orange flashes from the dying embers in our fireplace.

I guess it could happen anywhere, but the lingering lesson of the fisherman's walk and the dying embers is that soul mating is a process. It self-starts when the engine that drives productivity in the marketplace and at home is turned off.

LESLIE SR. AND LORA LEE PARROTT

❧ Prayer

Gracious God, refresh our lives with the strength of your Son. Let your presence be real in our minds and hearts. Direct us as we speak and listen. Help us to stay tuned in to our partner. Deepen our listening skills and guide us in ways we may become more sensitive to each other this week. Amen.

SESSION FORTY-TWO:
THE ATTITUDE
OF GRATITUDE

"Thanks," said Les. I had just handed him a stack of mail I picked up at his office.

"You bet," I replied without giving it a second thought.

"No, I mean it—thank you," Les said with all seriousness. "It was really thoughtful of you to pick up my mail and bring it home. You didn't have to do it, and I appreciate it."

It's always nice to be around somebody who's grateful. Cicero, the Roman philosopher, said, "Gratitude is not only the greatest of virtues, but the parent of all the others." When we are grateful—when we have an attitude of gratitude—we become better people.

Saying "thank you" tends to diminish over the years of marriage as we take each other more for granted. One group of social scientists discovered that the phrases "shhh" and "what's on" are more common in most homes than "thank you."

Scripture abounds with encouragement to be thankful. "Let the peace of Christ rule in your hearts, since as members of one body you were called to peace. And be *thankful*" (Col. 3:15, italics added). "*Giving thanks* to the Father, who has qualified you to share in the inheritance of the saints in the kingdom of light" (Col. 1:12, italics added). "Do not be anxious about anything, but in everything by prayer and petition, with *thanksgiving*, present your requests to God" (Phil. 4:6, italics added). The apostle Paul advised the church at Thessalonica: "*Give thanks* in all circumstances, for this is God's will for you in Christ Jesus" (1 Thess. 5:18, italics added). Scripture also tells us that thankfulness is a prerequisite for worship: "Enter his gates with *thanksgiving* and his courts with praise; give *thanks*" (Ps. 100:4, italics added).

To understand what it means to have the attitude of gratitude, we can start with a verse from the book of Hebrews. You may think at first that it has nothing to do with gratitude, but take a moment to read it.

> Therefore, since we are receiving a kingdom which cannot be shaken, let us have grace, by which we may serve God acceptably with reverence and godly fear. (Heb. 12:28 NKJV)

There is a remarkable difference between this translation of the passage and the translation found in the New International Version. Where the New King James Version says, "Let us have grace," the NIV says, "Let us be thankful." Each of these translations, however, is correct because in Greek, *charis*, "to have grace," also means "thank you."

Grace and thankfulness are connected. In giving thanks we receive grace. In other words, we cannot enjoy God's grace without being thankful. And we cannot be in good graces with our partner if we are not grateful.

So keep the attitude of gratitude alive in your marriage. Cultivate it by looking for things to appreciate in your partner each day. After all, gratitude really is the parent of all virtues.

FROM GOD'S WORD

Always try to be kind to each other and to everyone else. Be joyful always; pray continually; give thanks in all circumstances, for this is God's will for you in Christ Jesus.

1 THESSALONIANS 5:15–18

189

REAL-LIFE SOUL MATES

For Esther and me the best way to describe our life together is a covenant of love. We are both committed to walk as disciples of Christ, and this covenant binds us together in spirit, in purpose, and with integrity. Because of this common covenant, we have always been able to trust each other and to respect each other in our love as equally bearing the image of God.

Support for spirituality in our lives has come from reading the Word, from prayer, from worship, but especially from the dynamic of small group relationships. Over the past twenty-five years we have shared in three such groups. These have enriched us and stretched our spiritual resources by offering fellowship and demanding accountability. This has been especially true for the past thirteen years working in the inner city, where we have been participants in a "covenant group" of thirteen persons, meeting each Thursday evening for sharing. We've shared everything from personal issues to a careful review of one another's financial resources and patterns of stewardship. We must be willing to be vulnerable with others and to search all the corners of our spirits.

Once, during a time of deep anguish over a problem in our family, three persons from our group came and asked us to permit them to do the praying for us during the next week; we were to relax and unhook from the emotional burden of prayer on this issue! This was a level of participation in the Spirit that provided therapy for our own spirits.

In our ministry we frequently meet ourselves in other persons while studying, counseling, and serving. We have sought to avoid a professionalism that makes the spiritual into an expression more than an experience, and have regularly sought the infilling of the Spirit to enable us to walk together in the fellowship of Christ.

MYRON AND ESTHER AUGSBURGER

❧ Your Turn

- Many times the Scriptures talk about being thankful. Why do you think the virtue of gratitude is highlighted so often in the Bible?
- What is it about your partner that makes you the most thankful?
- Give an example of a recent time when your partner, out of courtesy, said "thank you" and it gave you a little boost.
- So often our gratitude goes unspoken. We feel grateful but we just don't say it. Share with your partner some "thank yous" you have been withholding.
- Take an inventory of the strengths of your marriage. How often do you give thanks to God for these gifts?

❧ Soul to Soul

To deepen your spiritual intimacy this next week, make note of:

- What you gained from this session together.
- A pressure point in your partner's upcoming week you will pray about.
- A concrete kindness you can offer your partner this week.

❧ Prayer

Generous Father, teach us day by day the deep rewards of gratitude. Help us to experience fully the gifts we have in one another—and enable us to make known our thankfulness to each other in such a way that it energizes and enriches our marriage this week. We thank you for all your blessings. Amen.

SESSION FORTY-THREE:
WHO'S IN CHARGE HERE?

Tim, a young man, recently married, invited me (Les) to lunch one day and asked, "How can I get my wife to submit to me?" His question threw me. I have counseled many newlyweds, but I had never heard the question phrased so bluntly.

Tim was a devout Christian trying to build his new marriage on biblical principles, and he wanted to be the "head" of the home. He read about headship in the verse that says, "The husband is the head of the wife as Christ is the head of the church, his body, of which he is the Savior" (Eph. 5:23). Tim interpreted this statement to mean literally that it was his job to be the boss of his wife. And it was her job to be submissive to his demands. Tim's wife, however, didn't see things that way because she lived in the twentieth century, not the first. She saw herself, understandably, as an equal partner in the marriage.

Tim, sincere as he was, didn't fully understand what it meant to be "the head of his wife as Christ is the head of the church." It never seemed to occur to Tim that in the Bible the husband is never called to make his wife submit. The Bible doesn't call husbands to rule over their wives but to renounce the desire to be master. Out of reverence for Christ, husbands should be the first to honor and respect their wives.

What then is headship? Let me tell you what I told Tim. Headship is not being the first in line. It is not being the boss or ruler. It is being the first to honor, the first to nurture, the first to meet your partner's needs.

A healthy marriage is built on a mutual desire to submit one's needs to the other. As Ephesians 5:21 says: "Submit to one another out of reverence for Christ." That's the basic principle. Emptying ourselves of our self-centered desires is the bridge to becoming soul mates. Without mutual submission every marriage, no matter how romantic, will eventually falter. As Amos 3:3 says, "Do two walk together unless they have agreed to do so?"

Remember the Aesop's fable in which the wind and the sun argued over which was the stronger? The wind said, "Do you see that old man down there? I can make him take his coat off quicker than you can."

The sun agreed to go behind a cloud while the wind blew up a storm. However, the harder the wind blew, the firmer the old man wrapped his coat around him. Eventually the wind gave up and the sun came out from behind the cloud and smiled kindly upon the old man. Before long, the man mopped his brow, pulled off his coat, and strolled along his way. The sun knew the secret: Warmth and a gentle touch are always stronger than force and fury.

If we worry about our partner submitting to us, we have not grasped this important principle. Like a blowing wind, our good intentions wreak havoc on our partner and our marriage. The key is understanding that submission is a two-way street in marriage. Scripture not only calls husbands and wives to "submit to one another" (Eph. 5:21), but we are to also submit to God (see Job 22:21; Heb. 12:9; James 4:7).

FROM GOD'S WORD

Wives, submit to your husbands as to the Lord. For the husband is the head of the wife as Christ is the head of the church, his body, of which he is the Savior. Now as the church submits to Christ, so also wives should submit to their husbands in everything.

Husbands, love your wives, just as Christ loved the church and gave himself up for her to make her holy, ... In this same way, husbands ought to love their wives as their own bodies. He who loves his wife loves himself.

EPHESIANS 5:22–26, 28 ❧

❧ Your Turn

- How does your faith enable you to practice mutual submission in your marriage and how does your marriage teach you about submitting to God?
- How was the principle of mutual submission modeled in your family growing up?
- It is difficult to submit to another's needs if you are unaware of them. Talk about how the two of you make your needs known to each other (i.e., are you direct, indirect, emotional, rational, etc.).
- Give an example of a time when each of you practiced mutual submission.
- In most marriages the wife makes some decisions, the husband makes others. But then there are some matters that are so important that they require both husband and wife. What are some examples of these important issues for you?

❧ Soul to Soul

To deepen your spiritual intimacy this next week, make note of:

- What you gained from this session together.
- A pressure point in your partner's upcoming week you will pray about.
- A concrete kindness you can offer your partner this week.

REAL-LIFE SOUL MATES

Both of us had prayed for a half-dozen years that we would "find love" with a spiritually sensitive person. When we met and married, we grounded the early years in morning Bible reading and prayer. When our sons came along, we added children's devotionals to the morning, eventually reading aloud segment-by-segment both Dorothy Sayers' *The Man Born to Be King* and Bruce Barton's *The Man Nobody Knows.* Now, for nearly ten years we have been reading a page of E. Stanley Jones' devotional books every day, polishing off one after Christmas every year. Don had received a gift of Jones' *The Way* as he left for college. He reports that reading that book through twice grounded him theologically and set his focus for spiritual formation.

We think our ripening spiritual sensitivity has brought us to celebrate our differences and our individual spiritual journeys, as well as to find daily strength in these anchoring sessions at breakfast time. Twenty years ago, we discovered we had a Genesis 3 marriage in which the woman's "desire" turns from God "to her husband," and the man accepts her challenge and flattery by making all of the decisions—"ruling over her." So we began to repent of our "fallen relationship" and to craft a different approach to the spiritual journey. Today we still do our anchor session every morning, but Robbie carries on extensive reading and reflecting every day, while Don does his personal inventory and accountability to God on his own. These are uniquely suited to our individual hungers, Don's need for dealing with internal issues and Robbie's extroversion which craves external stimulation. Most of all, we celebrate that we are profoundly grateful to have found both "couple" and "individual" expressions which are serving us so well today.

DON AND ROBBIE JOY

❧ Prayer

Merciful God, empty us of our self-centered desires and grant us the willingness to submit our needs to each other. Help us to discern the two-way street of mutual submission in our marriage as we build up our love and become soul mates. And God, teach us daily to submit to you. Amen.

SESSION FORTY-FOUR:
GOD'S PERFECT LOVE

In the opening scene of *Oliver*, the musical based on the Charles Dickens story of *Oliver Twist*, destitute boys in a London orphanage hover over a miserable meal of gruel. Meanwhile, the family and friends of the manager enjoy heaping platters of succulent fowl and tasty vegetables in an adjoining dining room that the boys can see. Although the paint is peeling on the stark gray wall behind the rough tables where the boys are sitting, a huge motto dares to show itself: GOD IS LOVE.

The audience is left to wonder whether the ragged, coughing urchins ever notice the dusty sign, let alone comprehend its meaning. But in reality, God's love is not part of a theatrical backdrop. It is not meant to have a paradoxical place onstage. God's love is real. It is living and breathing in you and your partner.

How you perceive God's love shapes your love for each other. God's love is self-sacrificing (John 15:13), unchangeable (John 13:1), and compelling (2 Cor. 5:14). God's love is also jealous (Exod. 20:5; 34:14; Deut. 4:25; 5:9; 6:15). This may sound strange to modern ears, but there is a beautiful idea behind this kind of "jealous" love. To say that God is a jealous God is to say that God is the lover of men and women, and that his heart can have no rival. He must have the whole devotion of our hearts. The divine-human relationship is not that of king and subject, nor that of master and servant, nor that of owner and slave, nor that of judge and defendant, but that of lover and loved one, a relationship which can only be paralleled in the perfect marriage relationship between husband and wife.

"When I stop to think of all that love should be—accepting, forgiving, supporting, strengthening—God is all that and more," writes Ruth Bell Graham. "He is perfect love." And when Ruth Graham feels that her love for her husband Billy does not measure up to such divine standards she says: "At that moment Romans 8:31–39 comes into my consciousness, and I am surrounded again by an awareness of God's love. He loves me in spite of me!"

Have you ever felt like your love is not all you want it to be? You're not alone. Only God's love is perfect. So as you begin the journey of becoming soul mates, pray that you will be "filled to the measure of all the fullness of God" (Eph. 3:19).

If the GOD IS LOVE sign had the audacity to cling to the scaly wall in Oliver's dreadful orphanage, it can surely abide in the hearts of a husband and wife who care for each other.

FROM GOD'S WORD

Who shall separate us from the love of Christ? Shall trouble or hardship or persecution or famine or nakedness or danger or sword? . . . No, in all these things we are more than conquerors through him who loved us. For I am convinced that neither death nor life, neither angels nor demons, neither the present nor the future, nor any powers, neither height nor depth, nor anything else in all creation, will be able to separate us from the love of God that is in Christ Jesus our Lord.

ROMANS 8:35–39 ❧

❧ Your Turn

- How does God's love, as expressed in the Romans passage, shape your love for your partner?
- Give an example of how you have recently encountered God's love living in your marriage through your partner's actions?

REAL-LIFE SOUL MATES

John, a young husband in our congregation, came to us one day filled with enthusiasm. He had discovered in Hebrews 4:15 that Jesus is "touched with our feelings." That expression from the old KJV had exploded like a holy light upon him and his wife, Ruby.

He exclaimed, "Pastor Jack and Anna, we've found a secret. Our arguments have suddenly begun to find quicker conclusions. Instead of analyzing what the other said, we've started *feeling*.

"I suddenly saw," he explained, "how Jesus feels the hurt of what bothers me, rather than complaining about my inadequacy or failure. This reminded me of Ephesians 5:25, and how it says I am to love my wife like Jesus loves the church."

This young man, ten years our junior, couldn't know how his insight helped us! And while our twenty years of marriage (at that time) had never held less than a full will to resolve all difficulties with loving commitment, something changed with our grasp of this concept. We found that *feelings*, not analyzing—the mind-wearying dissecting of words and meanings, situations and circumstances—cut more quickly to the core of problems in communication.

Now, when anything tough tests our patience with each other, we refuse to argue from logic, but rather allow ourselves to be "touched" with each other's feelings. Often, sitting with cups of tea at a winter fireside, we'll elaborate on the feelings we experienced—and the lessons they teach us about each other. The mood of such interchange is filled with discovery as we learn to be like Jesus toward each other—"touched with the feelings of our weaknesses."

JACK AND ANNA HAYFORD

- Discuss how God's love can sustain you in marriage even when one of you falls short of the mark on love.
- What is one way you and your partner can seek to become more "rooted and established in God's love"?
- Why do you think God's love is described as an "unchangeable" love? How does this inform your approach to loving your partner?

❧ Soul to Soul

To deepen your spiritual intimacy this next week, make note of:

- What you gained from this session together.
- A pressure point in your partner's upcoming week you will pray about.
- A concrete kindness you can offer your partner this week.

❧ Prayer

Gracious God, lover of our souls, we ask you to reveal your love to us as a couple. Show us your love for us as individuals through our partner's loving actions. And teach us to love as you do. We aspire to live a life that reflects your love, allowing you to transform our marriage into one of rare character. Thank you for a love from which nothing can separate us. Amen.

❧

Session Forty-Five:
The Guilt-Free Drop

In Les's book, *Love's Unseen Enemy*, he tells about learning to juggle. At a conference on laughter in the ballroom of the Disneyland Hotel, Dr. Steve Allen, Jr., the son of the famous comedian, handed out three scarves and then went through about a dozen steps to teach this room full of psychologists the art of juggling. The first step was to hold one of the scarves out at arm's length—and drop it.

Everyone thought he was joking. Nobody dropped their scarf. "C'mon now drop it!" Dr. Allen commanded. One by one, people reluctantly released their scarves and they fluttered to the carpeted floor. "There now, doesn't that feel better?" asked Dr. Allen. "You have gotten your mistake over with. This is the first step in learning to juggle. We call it the guilt-free drop."

Isn't that a wonderful principle? Do you need a guilt-free drop? Does your partner? Well, Les doesn't juggle that often, but we apply the guilt-free drop to our marriage almost daily.

Marriage offers a lot of opportunities for partners to feel guilty. In a survey assessing "who makes you feel most guilty," the majority of respondents confessed they were the key perpetrators of their own guilt. But next on the list was "my spouse."

Research has also revealed that much of the guilt we experience is undeserved. We endure false guilt when we suffer self-punishment needlessly. Our internal tape recorder says, "You should *always* have the house clean," "You should *never* come home late," or "You should *never* make a mistake."

Each of us is born with a judge and jury on the inside. We are in the courtroom daily, waiting to hear the verdict: Guilty or not guilty? Not that the decision has any bearing on the truth. It is our emotions, not reality, that will determine the verdict. For at the root of self-imposed guilt is the idea that what you feel must be true—or, in other words, if you *feel* guilty, you think you must have *done* something wrong. However, emotions can lie, because they are not products of reality, but of our *interpretation* of reality. The psalmist alludes to this when he says, "Troubles without number surround me; my sins have overtaken me, and I cannot see" (40:12).

Feelings of guilt cause blurry vision. That's why it is important for soul mates to give one another a guilt-free drop now and then. We need to offer grace to each other. We need to help each other see reality as it is, so that we can avoid needless self-punishment.

Of course, the saddest form of false guilt comes in not believing in and accepting God's grace and forgiveness. Paul writes to the Romans: "Therefore, there is now no condemnation for those who are in Christ Jesus, because through Christ Jesus the law of the Spirit of life set me free from the law of sin and death" (8:1). God sent his Son to earth not just to give us a guilt-free drop, but to give us a guilt-free life.

FROM GOD'S WORD

Even if I caused you sorrow by my letter, I do not regret it. Though I did regret it—I see that my letter hurt you, but only for a little while—yet now I am happy, not because you were made sorry, but because your sorrow led you to repentance. For you became sorrowful as God intended and so were not harmed in any way by us. Godly sorrow brings repentance that leads to salvation and leaves no regret, but worldly sorrow [guilt] brings death.

2 CORINTHIANS 7:8–10 ❧

REAL-LIFE SOUL MATES

Many Christian marriages claim to be highly successful with glowing romance and delight on a consistent basis. In some thirty years of psychiatric practice, I've learned that not all Christian marriages are so idyllic. Ours has been one of the more realistic kind. Sure, we have enjoyed many idyllic periods in our nearly forty-five-year relationship, but we have also suffered turbulence by, knowingly or not, inflicting great pain on one another.

In the immense or minuscule conflicts of our marriage, our greatest growth emerged from the heartbreak of these times, and we came to understand the real definition of redemption. Christ has gently, and sometimes fiercely, intruded into our turmoil with his command to forgive each other as he forgave us. By bending our strong wills to obey him, we learned the peace and indescribable love of reconciliation through forgiving. And genuine forgiving must also include forgetting. Someone has wisely said that those who forgive, but never let the other forget that they forgave, fall short of the genuine.

One of the great blessings of our lives is the certainty that each frequently prays for the other. We pray for safety and health, an especially important prayer as we age. We pray for wisdom and for God to use us in our daily work. The knowledge of such specific prayers is not only comforting and endearing, but empowering.

Through obedience, we have known that intimate presence of Christ, himself, in daily events. Our priorities have become rearranged and we value one another to a depth we once thought impossible.

HERBERT AND GRACE KETTERMAN

❧ Your Turn

- Some Christians believe that God wants them to feel guilty. Do you have a hard time believing that there is "no condemnation for those who are in Christ Jesus"?
- Give an example of a time in your life when you were afforded grace instead of guilt. What did that do for you?
- Discuss the difference between true guilt and false guilt and how both affect marriage?
- When are you most tempted to make your mate feel guilty? Why?
- Talk about some real-life situations where you might give one another a "guilt-free drop"?

❧ Soul to Soul

To deepen your spiritual intimacy this next week, make note of:

- What you gained from this session together.
- A pressure point in your partner's upcoming week you will pray about.
- A concrete kindness you can offer your partner this week.

❧ Prayer

Our Father, help us to live in the fullness and light of your salvation rather than under the dark shadow of guilt. Lift the quality of our life together. Show us your grace daily in our lives and teach us to give ourselves to each other. Grant us a marriage without condemnation. Amen.

STOP STEWING AND START DOING

A University of Michigan study determined that sixty percent of human worries are totally unwarranted. Of the remaining portion of our worries, twenty percent are about things already past and activities completely beyond our control. Another ten percent are so petty that they don't make much difference at all. Of the remaining ten percent of our worries, only four to five percent are really justifiable. And even half of this residue of viable worries is beyond our capacity to change! The final half, or two percent of our worries which are real, can be solved easily, according to these researchers, "if we stop stewing and start doing!"

The precision of these statistics is not important. The indisputable point is that most of our worries are not worth the stress they generate. How many times have the two of you let worry cloud your dinner conversation? How often do you lie awake at night consumed with an obsessive worry?

You don't have to let the poison of worry contaminate your marriage. God wants to cleanse you from needless concerns. Long ago the apostle Paul wrote that we are to stop perpetually worrying about even one thing. And he gave us a prescription for inoculating ourselves against worry in Philippians 4:4–7:

> Rejoice in the Lord always. I will say it again: Rejoice! Let
> your gentleness be evident to all. The Lord is near. Do not
> be anxious about anything, but in everything, by prayer and

petition, with thanksgiving, present your requests to God. And the peace of God, which transcends all understanding, will guard your hearts and your minds in Christ Jesus.

You want to be free from worry? Bring your concerns to God with an attitude of thanksgiving. Don't try to figure out everything. How this prescription for worry sickness works, Paul says, is beyond understanding. But be assured of this, it does work.

Jesus Christ came to give us eternal life, but also *abundant* life (see John 10:10). He came to give us life to the fullest and to set us free from the harmful effects of worry. By the way, Jesus practiced what he preached. When faced with the hostility of Herod and the pressure of the public clamor for healing, for example, he had plenty to worry about. Instead, Scripture tells us, he and the disciples took rest. Jesus said to his disciples: "Come with me by yourselves to a quiet place and get some rest" (Mark 6:31).

So don't allow worry to get a foothold in your marriage. Life is too short. The possibilities are too great. Instead, as soul mates, you can help each other to "cast all your anxiety on him because he cares for you" (1 Peter 5:7).

FROM GOD'S WORD

Then Jesus said to his disciples: "Therefore I tell you, do not worry about your life, what you will eat; or about your body, what you will wear. Life is more than food, and the body more than clothes. Consider the ravens: They do not sow or reap, they have no storeroom or barn; yet God feeds them. And how much more valuable you are than birds! Who of you by worrying can add a single hour to his life? Since you cannot do this very little thing, why do you worry about the rest?

LUKE 12:22–26 ❧

REAL-LIFE SOUL MATES

As parents of active young children, we find that often daily crises interfere with our attempts to have a scheduled spiritual life with each other. So we have learned to use the needs, problems, and joys of each day to bring ourselves and our children closer to God.

Once, at two in the morning, John drove three-year-old Ricky to the emergency room as a code three croup, gasping for breath with blocked airways. God was our only hope, and we found ourselves drawn much closer to him and each other. We often point to that event as a time we learned much about actively depending on him.

Often we see God through our children. Once, two-year-old Benny slipped away from Barbi at a large school gathering. Panicked, she searched until she finally found him toddling in a hallway, lost in a sea of grown-up legs and torsos. When Benny spotted Barbi, he wailed and held up his arms for her to rescue him. Later, when Barbi told John the story, we were moved by how much like Benny ourselves are: needing God's presence and comfort.

We're always concerned with what we're transferring to our next generation: Will it be our sins and dysfunctional patterns or our mature character traits? One night, as our two sons fought in the kitchen, we worried about their "bad attitudes," that is, until we realized that their squabbling style was identical to ours! As we realize our twofold task of stopping generational sin patterns and developing mature character in our kids, we feel much more of a need to confess, repent, and ask forgiveness for our own immaturities.

We struggle as imperfect, unfinished parents, asking God and each other to help us grow each other up so we can help our boys grow up.

JOHN AND BARBI TOWNSEND

❧ Your Turn

- Why does Scripture tell us to not be anxious about anything?
- In what ways has your marriage suffered as a result of worry?
- What recurring issues tend to cause the most anxiety and worry for each of you?
- Give an example of a time when you experienced peace rather than anxiety in the face of fearful circumstances. What made it so?
- How can you help each other release worry and rely on Christ for peace and provision?

❧ Soul to Soul

To deepen your spiritual intimacy this next week, make note of:

- What you gained from this session together.
- A pressure point in your partner's upcoming week you will pray about.
- A concrete kindness you can offer your partner this week.

❧ Prayer

God, we acknowledge the frailty of our humanness by the unnecessary load of worry we carry. Teach us a way to live without self-defeating worry. Thank you for bearing our burdens. Help us to live in more peace and tranquillity than we did last week and the week before. Help us find the more excellent way. Amen.

SESSION FORTY-SEVEN:

SINKING YOUR ROOTS
DOWN DEEP

If you are like most couples in America, you won't live in one place very long. In an average year, some forty million Americans move. Put another way, every ten years, between forty and sixty percent of an average American town's population moves in or out. And get this. The average worker only keeps a job 3.6 years. So will you lengthen your roots and stay where you are for a good long while? Probably not. If you are like most Americans, you will move about fourteen times in your lifetime.

Of course multiple moves have not always characterized life in America. Chances are that your grandparents or great-grandparents stayed most of their adult lives in the same region, even the same house. Before our country was crisscrossed with interstate highways and before airplanes made cross-country travel easy, people stayed put a lot more than we do now. People had deep roots.

You have to work pretty hard in our high-tech society to lay down lifelong roots. It's not impossible, but it's rare. However, there is a kind of rootedness in marriage that comes from being soul mates. Allow us to illustrate it this way: The root system of most trees is as wide and deep as the leaf line is wide and high. That is not true, however, of the redwood, which has a shallow root system that spreads out in all directions. That fact of life creates a problem for a redwood standing alone. It can easily be blown over because the lack of deep roots gives it little stability. However when two redwoods grow together, their root structures intertwine with each other and give one another strength. Though weak as separate trees, they become strong together. The same is true for soul mates. "Two are better than one," said King Solomon (Eccl. 4:9).

Whether you live in one place for many years or relocate around the country according to job requirements, the most important roots you'll ever establish are in God and his Word. For this spiritual root system will bear much fruit. "I am the vine," said Jesus, "you are the branches. If a man remains in me and I in him, he will bear much fruit; apart from me you can do nothing.... If you remain in me and my words remain in you, ask whatever you wish, and it will be given you. This is to my Father's glory, that you bear much fruit, showing yourselves to be my disciples" (John 15:5–8).

As a couple grows together in their understanding of God and his Word, they become all the more "rooted and established in love" (Eph. 3:17). So if your circumstances take you from coast to coast or anywhere around the world, never forget that soul mates, like the redwoods, become stronger together.

FROM GOD'S WORD

Two are better than one, because they have a good return for their work: If one falls down, his friend can help him up. But pity the man who falls and has no one to help him up! Also, if two lie down together, they will keep warm. But how can one keep warm alone? Though one may be overpowered, two can defend themselves. A cord of three strands is not quickly broken.

ECCLESIASTES 4:9–12 ❧

❧ Your Turn

- Christ invites us to "abide in him." What does this mean to you and how does it nurture your spiritual root system?

REAL-LIFE SOUL MATES

I don't know of many husbands who can claim that their wives make them better monks. But I can. As founders of an integrated monastery, we are part of a community that participates daily in spiritual disciplines.

Viola and I first experienced the spiritual intimacy that characterizes soul mates during times of extended prayer—two to three hours sped by as if it were only fifteen minutes. And it was these experiences, along with a growing conviction that we were following God's will, that convinced us, two avowed celibates, to seek counsel and eventually join in a marriage blessed by the church.

As a couple, we participate in the ongoing disciplines of the monastic community: poverty, mental chastity, and obedience. And silence. From morning until noon each day, we share a "sacred silence" during which we speak only as love demands and always in a soft voice. We also regularly share night prayers, or compline, together before retiring. This is a ten-minute spiritual exercise that incorporates an examination of the conscience (for the activities and attitudes of the day), the reading of a psalm, and a sprinkling with holy water. We have found that when the last thoughts before sleep are holy, wholesome, and beautiful, it sets the tone for the next day.

JOHN MICHAEL AND VIOLA TALBOT

- Most married couples experience times of uprooting from family or friends. What has your experience been?
- Give an example of a project or activity or experience which has "intertwined your roots" as soul mates.
- What are the goals you share as a couple that increase your rootedness in each other?
- How are the two of you growing together in an understanding of God's Word? Can you think of some specific examples?

❧ Soul to Soul

To deepen your spiritual intimacy this next week, make note of:

- What you gained from this session together.
- A pressure point in your partner's upcoming week you will pray about.
- A concrete kindness you can offer your partner this week.

❧ Prayer

Gracious God, the blessings that come from being rooted together in your Word are many. You have promised to make us fruitful and prosperous and to protect us from withering in the face of adversity. Teach us to delight in your Word and to draw strength from one another. Enable us to drop our roots into the rich soil of a good marriage relationship and to be established in strength together. Amen.

❧

DO YOU DREAM
WHAT I DREAM?

The musical play *Man of La Mancha* is one of our all-time favorites. It is the story of a crazy old man suffering from what we would now call senile psychosis.

The action takes place a hundred years after the age of chivalry when there were no more knights. But, thinking he is one, Don Quixote puts on a strange suit of armor and rides into the world to battle evil and protect the weak and powerless. He brings along his funny, little servant Sancho Panza as his squire. When they arrive at a broken-down old inn used by mule traders, Don Quixote calls the innkeeper the lord of a great castle. In the inn he meets the most miserable human being imaginable, a pathetic orphan girl who does menial chores and is degraded by the mule traders. Don Quixote pronounces this wretched girl the great lady Dulcinea and begs for her handkerchief as a token to carry with him into battle.

Everyone thinks Don Quixote is bonkers, but at the end of the play the old, dying man no longer suffers from these delusions. In a moving scene, all the people he has renamed appear at his bedside and beg him not to change. His excitement about their future has transformed them and they have become the people that this insane visionary imagined.

The message of the play is simple: The dreams and hopes of the people around us powerfully shape our lives. And the message to married couples is that what you dream for each other (and whether you dream) will powerfully shape your marriage.

We have a plaque in our home with the following inscription from Henry David Thoreau: "If one advances confidently in the direction of his dreams, and endeavors to live the life which he has imagined, he will meet with a success unexpected in common hours." What we consciously dream about, what we envision for our future together, and the goals we set for our partnership, determine the quality of our marriage in the present. For where there is no vision, a marriage will perish (see Prov. 29:18). And if our dreams are worthy and filled with godly hope they take us to heights we never imagined.

Of course, it is possible to have dreams that are not godly. So how should a Christian couple dream according to the Bible? Consider a paraphrasing of Paul's words in Philippians 4:8: "Whatever is true, whatever is noble, whatever is right, whatever is pure, whatever is lovely, whatever is admirable—dream on those things." The focus of a healthy dream and vision is not on "laying up treasures on earth" but on pleasing God.

So learn to dream. And dream big! It was H. W. K. Moule who rightly said, "The frontiers of the Kingdom of God were never advanced by men and women of caution."

FROM GOD'S WORD

The eye is the lamp of the body. If your eyes are good, your whole body will be full of light. But if your eyes are bad, your whole body will be full of darkness. If then the light within you is darkness, how great is that darkness!

MATTHEW 6:22–23 ❧

❧ Your Turn

- Scripture underscores the value of dreams and visions again and again. Why do you think this is?

Real-Life Soul Mates

When we first attended Marriage Encounter in 1976, I realized I had allowed our marriage to drift. I was taking my wife, Harriet, for granted. I was doing nothing consciously to strengthen our commitment to one another. We had been married ten years, had three sons, and were active in a spiritually nurturing church. But I had become so involved in my work that I spent little time with her, and I was doing nothing to nurture her as a person.

Paul, in his letter to the Ephesians, states what I now recognize as the cardinal principle for making marriage strong: "Submit to one another out of reverence for Christ." During the first ten years of our marriage, Harriet was submitting to me, but I was not submitting to her. As in many marriages, my wife was a giver, and I was a taker.

"You love your work more than you love me. You are neither a husband nor a father," she said on our Marriage Encounter. Her opinion shocked me. However, when I looked at how many hours I was working—and how little time I was spending with her or with our boys—I realized that I needed to change.

Marriage Encounter recommended that we devote twenty minutes every day exclusively to each other. I resolve to do that. Each morning, we rise a little earlier than our demands of the day require. We begin by simply talking about whatever it is that we are concerned about. We enjoy coffee, observe the changing trees through our bedroom skylight, or watch birds at a feeder outside our window. Then I read from a couple-commentary and from Scripture. For years, I have simply read a chapter of Proverbs. There are exactly thirty-one chapters of Proverbs—which I see as one for every day of the month. If today is the twelfth of the month, I'll read Chapter 12, and we will always find the mind of the Lord on how to build a marital relationship.

Mike and Harriet McManus

- Give an example of a time when your partner was a catalyst for something beyond your expectations—a time when he or she helped you dream.
- What are the dreams you share for your future together? How do you see your marriage, ten, twenty, thirty years from now?
- Sometimes a spouse will unknowingly shoot down a partner's dream. Has this happened to either of you? How can you prevent this from happening?
- Have you ever written down goals as a couple? If you were to note three goals for your marriage what would they be?

❧ Soul to Soul

To deepen your spiritual intimacy this next week, make note of:
- What you gained from this session together.
- A pressure point in your partner's upcoming week you will pray about.
- A concrete kindness you can offer your partner this week.

❧ Prayer

God of all knowledge, fill our lives with vision which is beyond this moment or this week. Help us to dream expansively for the future of our life together. May we challenge and support one another in such a way that our dreams elevate our partner to a better life. Thank you for your promise to withhold no good thing from us. We are grateful for your goodness and mercy. Amen.

SESSION FORTY-NINE:
A LITTLE HEAVEN ON EARTH

There is a story of a man who dreamed that he died and found himself immediately in a large room. In the room there was a huge banquet table filled with all sorts of delicious food. Around the banquet table were people seated on chairs, obviously hungry. But the chairs were five feet from the edge of the table and the people apparently could not get out of the chairs. Furthermore, their arms were not long enough to reach the food on the table.

In the dream there was one large spoon, five feet long. Everyone was fighting, quarreling, pushing each other, trying to grab hold of that spoon. Finally, in an awful scene, one strong bully got hold of the spoon. He reached out, picked up some food, and turned it to feed himself, only to find that the spoon was so long he could not touch his mouth. The food fell off. Immediately, someone else grabbed the spoon and held it. The new owner reached to pick up the food, but again could not feed himself. The handle was too long.

In the dream, the man who was observing it all said to his guide, "This is hell—to have food and not be able to eat it." The guide replied, "Where do you think you are? This *is* hell. But this is not your place. Come with me."

And they went into another room. In this room there was also a long table filled with food, exactly as in the other room. Everyone was seated in chairs, and for some reason they, too, seemed unable to get out of their chairs.

Like the others, they were unable to reach the food on the table. Yet they had a satisfied, pleasant look on their faces. Only then did the visitor see the reason why. Exactly as before, there was only one spoon. It, too, had a handle five feet long. Yet no one was fighting for it. In fact, one man, who held the handle, reached out, picked up the food, and put it into the mouth of someone else, who ate it and was satisfied.

That person then took the spoon by the handle, reached for the food from the table, and put it to the mouth of the man who had just given him something to eat. And the guide said, "This is heaven."

There is a good message for soul mates in this allegory. You can create a little heaven on earth by helping each other get your needs met. By working in cooperation with one another, your own home can be a taste of heavenly blessings (see Eph. 1:3, 20; 2:6; 3:10).

In the great prayer that Jesus taught his disciples he says: "Our Father in heaven, hallowed be your name, your kingdom come, your will be done on earth as it is in heaven" (Matt. 6:9–10). The implication is that our lives can enjoy a foretaste of heaven. Christ would not teach his followers a prayer that could not be fulfilled.

In the garden area behind our home, which is built on a steep slope, there is a large retaining wall. And on the top of this tall wall is a small statuary angel that sits on the corner and looks over us. It's a pretty sculpture, but it serves as more than a piece of art to us. Our retaining wall angel is a reminder that in our marriage we can have a little heaven right here on earth. And so can you.

FROM GOD'S WORD

Praise be to the God and Father of our Lord Jesus Christ, who has blessed us in the heavenly realms with every spiritual blessing in Christ. For he chose us in him before the creation of the world to be holy and blameless in his sight.

EPHESIANS 1:3–4

REAL-LIFE SOUL MATES

Our spiritual oneness began when we started dating. Jim was looking for a spiritual woman as a wife—in fact, he talked to me about my spiritual life on our first date. The first night of our marriage we read Scripture and prayed together. We also started other habits, such as praying together before meals and praying aloud on the spot when a special concern arose for ourselves or for others.

Over the years our "official" devotional times have had to change. When it was just the two of us, our quiet times could be fixed, but the schedule needed to be flexible when we had children. Now that our children have grown and left home, we enjoy reading various devotional books at breakfast and praying for our friends around the world.

Despite these changes, we have maintained a ritual of praying together just before going off to sleep, and this has had the greatest impact on our spiritual intimacy. This is when we draw together, honestly laying our problems and joys before God. We have prayed through frightening times when one of our daughters was very ill or injured. Always, we felt God's peace by holding onto each other in prayer.

We always prayed that Christ would be formed in each of our girls so that they would be women of God in an alien world. When we both went through tough midlife crises, we prayed not so much *with* each other as *for* each other. In recent years we've shared prayer daily for Sally's physical health as she battles with breast cancer and the debilitating effects of chemotherapy.

Life has given us many times to choose to build spiritual intimacy or to isolate and lick our wounds in private. We weren't born "soul mates"—but we became soul mates as we cared for each other through all the seasons of life.

JIM AND SALLY CONWAY

❧ Your Turn

- Do you have any tangible reminders in your home that serve as an impetus for creating a little heaven on earth through your marriage?
- What selfish pattern do you see in yourself that you would like to change? How does it impact your marriage?
- How do you work cooperatively to meet each other's needs? Give some examples.
- What is a concrete step each of you can take right now to initiate a pattern of increased kindness in your marriage?
- Are there areas of your life where you are ruggedly independent or reluctant to accept help? Share with your partner how he or she can offer the type of assistance you desire.

❧ Soul to Soul

To deepen your spiritual intimacy this next week, make note of:

- What you gained from this session together.
- A pressure point in your partner's upcoming week you will pray about.
- A concrete kindness you can offer your partner this week.

❧ Prayer

Holy God, make us eager to give to one another. Help us to possess kindness toward each other in increasing measure. Enable us to work cooperatively to enjoy a foretaste of heaven in our home this very moment. This we pray with assurance, amen.

SESSION FIFTY:
A MILE IN MARRIAGE MOCCASINS

Rarely a month goes by that we do not receive a wedding invitation. And leading up to the month of June our mailbox seems to overflow. Because of our work with engaged couples, we attend a lot of weddings. And many of the weddings we attend include the traditional candle ceremony at some point in the service, usually near the end. The bride and groom each take a burning candle and light another candle, then blow out their own candles, symbolizing that the two have become one.

Every time we observe the lighting of a unity candle, however, we are reminded that marriage doesn't work like that. No one can blow out his or her personality, let alone that of his or her partner. Even after years of marriage, partners remain uniquely themselves. That's one of the big reasons why marriage is an ongoing challenge—and an adventure!

We hope you respect one another's individuality and uniqueness. Too many couples believe being married means being alike. And that causes problems. For it leads us to *expect* our spouse to be just like us, and when he or she isn't—which is most of the time—we become critical.

There is an old Sioux Indian prayer that gets at the solution to this common problem. It says: "Oh Great Spirit, grant me the wisdom to walk in another's moccasins before I criticize or pass judgment." Learning to walk in your mate's moccasins is at the heart of a healthy marriage relationship. Psychologists call it empathy, the rare capacity to put ourselves into the shoes of our partner and accurately see life from his or her perspective.

Empathy combines two important capacities: to analyze and to sympathize, to use our heads and to use our hearts. Our analytical capacities involve collecting facts and observing conditions. We look at a problem, we break it down into its causes, and we propose solutions. That's analyzing. Sympathizing is feeling for another person. It is feeling the pain of someone who is suffering or feeling the anger of a person in rage. Sympathizing and analyzing are the twin engines of empathy. One without the other is fine, but their true power is found in combination. We need to love with both our head and our heart to empathize.

The apostle Paul encouraged empathy in Hebrews when he said: "Remember those in prison as if you were their fellow prisoners, and those who are mistreated as if you yourselves were suffering" (13:3). He also said, "We who are strong ought to bear with the failings of the weak and not to please ourselves" (Rom. 15:1).

When we empathize with our partner, we put aside our expectation that he or she should be like us. We accept the fact that our partner has brought unique personality into our marriage and we ask ourselves questions like "What is *he* feeling? What pressures does *she* have to cope with? What does *he* fear? What does *she* need? How, if at all, should I help my spouse?"

The best model of empathy is our Lord himself. If Jesus Christ had been merely sympathetic to our plight, he would have watched our struggles from afar, shaking his head and feeling bad. If he had been merely analytical, he would have told us exactly what to do, stripping us of our freedom and solving all our problems for us. Instead, the Son of God chose to become one of us (see John 1:14; Luke 1:32; Phil. 2:7; Col. 1:15; 1 Tim 2:5).

So before you jump to conclusions, before you criticize, before you pass judgment, use Jesus as your model and walk in your partner's shoes.

FROM GOD'S WORD

Each of you should look not only to your own interests, but also to the interests of others. Your attitude should be the same as that of Christ Jesus: Who, being in very nature God, did not consider equality with God something to be grasped, but made himself nothing, taking the very nature of a servant, being made in human likeness. And being found in appearance as a man, he humbled himself and became obedient to death—even death on a cross!

PHILIPPIANS 2:4–8 ❧

❧ Your Turn

- While the word "empathy" is never used in the Bible, it is, in a sense, what the whole Gospel message is about. Talk about the way empathy is ultimately demonstrated in the life of Christ.
- What is one of the areas where you would especially like your spouse to empathize with you?
- It is easy to jump to conclusions and become critical without first understanding why our mate did something. What would allow you to catch yourself the next time you are tempted to do so?
- In what ways have you consciously or unconsciously wished your partner was more like you? Are you ready to let that expectation go?
- Give an example of a time you consciously tried to empathize with your partner. Was it hard work? What happened as a result of your effort?

REAL-LIFE SOUL MATES

For us, spiritual intimacy has been created in our mutual struggle for justice. Both of us are committed to working for the liberating of oppressed people. Over the years, we have developed a variety of ministries for inner-city teenagers and children. They have included programs in sex education, literacy, job training, and Bible study. The ministry has involved a lot of sweat and a lot of tears, for we have shared in the sufferings of the children we try to reach.

Such concern drives us to our knees and develops a spirituality built on mutual concerns. In the Scriptures we read about entering into "the fellowship of his sufferings." Certainly, we have learned something about the spiritual fellowship that comes when we allow our hearts to be broken.

Over the last few years, Peggy and I have been reaching out to our homosexual brothers and sisters as well. They have cried out for the church to show compassion and love. Specifically, we are concerned about those who are suffering from AIDS. We pray for them and try to sensitize the church to care for them. We do not justify the sexual promiscuity that often leads to this dreaded disease, but we cry out to the church to show the same compassion to them that was shown by Christ to the lepers in his day. They also were people with a disease that was marked with spiritual and moral connotations, yet Jesus touched them and loved them and let them know that through him they still had a place in the kingdom of God.

As we have sought to express that kind of love, we have been misunderstood, hurt, and attacked. But to share in such sufferings fosters intimacy. In fact, we've never felt closer to each other at any other time in our marriage.

TONY AND PEGGY CAMPOLO

⅔ Soul to Soul

To deepen your spiritual intimacy this next week, make note of:

- What you gained from this session together.
- A pressure point in your partner's upcoming week you will pray about.
- A concrete kindness you can offer your partner this week.

⅔ Prayer

Christ Jesus, open the eyes of our hearts and the ears of our minds to grant true empathy to our partner. Teach us to put ourselves in each other's shoes. Help us to identify one another's feelings, pressures, fears, and needs. And help us to do those things that make life better for each other. Amen.

SESSION FIFTY-ONE:

THE QUESTION THAT COULD CHANGE YOUR MARRIAGE

The oddsmakers say the chances are five in ten that a marriage will end in divorce. If one or both partners are still teenagers, they say the odds for divorce are even higher. If either partner witnessed an unhappy marriage at home, the odds increase again. If one or both partners come from broken homes, the odds rise yet higher. If either partner has been divorced, the odds soar. If there has been regular sexual involvement before marriage, or if either or both partners abuse alcohol or drugs, the odds skyrocket.

Well, regardless of your marriage "odds," we have a soul-searching question for you that will help you beat them. Are you ready? Ask yourself: *How would I like to be married to me?*

That simple question can do more to help you ensure the success of your marriage than just about anything else. Think about it. How would you rate *you* as a marriage partner? Are you easy to live with? How do you enrich the relationship? What are the positive qualities you bring to your marriage?

Learn the lesson Paul wrote about in 2 Corinthians: "We do not dare to classify or compare ourselves with some who commend themselves. When they measure themselves by themselves and compare themselves with themselves, they are not wise" (10:12).

Every marriage is unique, and while there is no definitive list of qualities that describe good spouses, consider some of the traits that show up again and again in studies of lifelong love. Research, for example, has shown that partners who are easy to live with feel good about themselves. They are not unduly concerned over the impression they make on others. They can throw back their heads, breathe deep, and enjoy life. This kind of person is described in Galatians: "... he can take pride in himself, without comparing himself to somebody else" (6:4). People who make good lifelong marriage partners also have a way of passing over minor offenses and injustices. In other words, they are not easily offended (see Rom. 14:20; Prov. 17:9). Some spouses punish their partner with time in the penalty box for ordinary bruises which happen to people who play the game.

Partners who are easy to live with are cooperative. They get along. They understand what the psalmist meant in saying, "How good and pleasant it is [to] live together in unity" (133:1; see also Acts 4:32; Rom. 14:19). They also have an even and stable emotional tone. Nobody is attracted to an uncontrollable temper (see James 1:19–20). Good spouses communicate their needs openly and honestly (see Eph. 4:15). What they say is in sync with how they feel and what they want. They do not mask their feelings to protect their pride or even to avoid hurting their spouse's feelings. Instead, they share their innermost thoughts, the good and the bad (see Col. 3:12).

You may not have every advantage for a successful marriage, few do. But you can pray with the psalmist: "Search me, O God, and know my heart" (139:23). By searching your soul, by questioning your character, and by becoming easy to live with, you will exponentially increase the probability of making your marriage last a lifetime. Paul says that people who are easy to live with shine like stars in the universe (see Phil. 2:15).

FROM GOD'S WORD

For this very reason, make every effort to add to your faith goodness; and to goodness, knowledge; and to knowledge, self-control; and to self-control, perseverance; and to perseverance, godliness; and to godliness, brotherly kindness; and to brotherly kindness, love. For if you possess these qualities in increasing measure, they will keep you from being ineffective and unproductive in your knowledge of our Lord Jesus Christ.

2 PETER 1:5–8 ❧

❧ Your Turn

- The Bible lists many admirable qualities, virtues, and traits. Out of the ones mentioned in the passage from 2 Peter, which ones do you find toughest to practice?
- Share with your partner how you think you might be difficult to live with at times. What qualities would make it hard for you to be married to you?
- Share with your partner the qualities he or she possesses that make it easy for you to be married to him or her.
- What makes it so difficult for most spouses to pass over minor offenses in marriage?
- Talk about one thing each of you is going to work on this week to become easier to live with.

❧ Soul to Soul

To deepen your spiritual intimacy this next week, make note of:

- What you gained from this session together.
- A pressure point in your partner's upcoming week you will pray about.
- A concrete kindness you can offer your partner this week.

REAL-LIFE SOUL MATES

The early years of our marriage were ones filled with turmoil. We struggled so much with working out our differences that we allowed our conflicts to consume our energy, leaving nothing for the development of spiritual intimacy. It wasn't that we didn't know it was to be the foundation of our relationship, it was just too easy for us to get caught up with the issues of family, growing active boys, and the work of ministry. We made certain we spent time with our children, teaching them spiritual principles and praying with them, but we struggled with praying together, just the two of us.

On the surface, one would think that praying together would be easy, especially since I had been a pastor for several years. We both grew up in Christian homes and learned early how to pray with others. I could pray in church services, at meetings, or even with other people in my office. But praying with my wife presented a whole different experience internally for me. Jan was open and ready, but I was resistive and fearful.

Finally, we simply decided that we would begin to pray together every night before we went to bed. It was the willful resolve to do it that finally broke through whatever fears of vulnerability or intimacy lay within me. We started simply by praying for our family members and for each other.

Over the years our prayer time has expanded and become the major building block within our lives and our marriage. When we are apart, we make sure we have time to pray together over the phone. Our prayer time has become so much a part of our relationship that it is natural for us to interrupt our conversation with "Let's pray about this." Comfort and intimacy with each other have been built by the consistent practice of sharing together that important spiritual discipline of prayer.

DAVID AND JAN STOOP

❧ Prayer

Our God and Father, we long to know you more and serve you better. For it is only in relationship with you that our love for each other can truly grow. Help us to keep in mind who we are in this partnership. Show us the way to become better marriage partners. Help us to work on those qualities that bring glory to you and joy to each other. Strengthen us by your Spirit for every good work. Amen.

Session Fifty-Two:
Soul to Soul
Forever and Ever

Last summer our family gathered around a large circular table in an elegant restaurant that has unofficially become the backdrop for many of our most meaningful family celebrations. For decades, literally, our family has gathered here from around the country to mark holidays, birthdays, graduations, promotions, and farewells. But this time was different. The dinner was a celebration of mom and dad's fiftieth wedding anniversary. They didn't want a big party. This celebration was strictly a family affair.

The food, as always, was exquisite. The anniversary cake was lovely. The presents were nice, but not worthy of such a noble occasion. What impressed us most about the entire event, however, wasn't tangible. It was something my father said. We had just offered grace and thanked God for the family and the many years Mom and Dad had lived together. Then, before picking up his fork, he looked around the table and said: "I can't believe it has been fifty years! The time is so short!"

The rest of the meal was devoted to reminiscing. Mom talked about the times when each of her three sons was born. She could describe in detail the various homes we lived in. Dad talked about the churches and colleges he and Mom had served. There was the first pastorate they took during the Korean War and the transition to being a college president during the Mid-East oil crisis. They both reminisced about their first trip to London and many other journeys around the globe. They must certainly have had some hard times, like all married couples do, but all they seemed to remember were things they enjoyed together.

Fifty years! What will your marriage look like in fifty years? What will you reminisce about? Can you imagine your future together? "There is surely a future hope for you, and your hope will not be cut off" (Prov. 23:18).

"By wisdom a house is built," says Proverbs, "and through understanding it is established; through knowledge its rooms are filled with rare and beautiful treasures" (24:3–4). After fifty years, what memorable treasures will your house of love include?

Something else struck us about Mom and Dad's fiftieth wedding anniversary—their utter dependence on God. It is impossible to separate their spiritual formation from their marital maturity. They are living proof to us that no single factor does more to cultivate oneness and a meaningful sense of purpose in marriage than a shared commitment to spiritual discovery.

Sharing life's ultimate meaning with another person is the call of soul mates. Spirituality is to your marriage as yeast is to a loaf of bread. We have said to hundreds of couples: Ultimately, your spiritual commitment will determine whether your marriage rises successfully or falls disappointingly flat.

Will you look back while celebrating fifty years of marriage and say, "I can't believe time is so short"? We pray you will. For, "As a bridegroom rejoices over his bride, so will your God rejoice over you" (Isa. 62:5).

FROM GOD'S WORD

I will betroth you to me forever; I will betroth you in righteousness and justice, in love and compassion. I will betroth you in faithfulness, and you will acknowledge the LORD.

HOSEA 2:19–20 ❧

REAL-LIFE SOUL MATES

First of all, we have never felt a great need to have a regular devotional time together. There have been times when we felt a little bit envious of those who did—like maybe we were missing out on something really important. But despite those occasional pangs of envy or even guilt, we haven't made an effort to "do devotions" together on a regular basis.

Still, we do enjoy spiritual intimacy. That doesn't mean we are always discussing spiritual matters or praying together. There are times when we do that, but those times are relatively infrequent and always unpredictable (making them all the more wonderful). Instead, we encourage and allow each other to spend time alone with God, and we participate together in worship and spiritual growth in community with the church. We approach God in very different ways (our personalities are quite different) and we respect each other's need for spiritual privacy. In a sense, it is spiritual privacy which contributes to a deeper intimacy between us when we share our spiritual journeys with each other.

In addition to our church involvement, we share many other opportunities for spiritual growth, such as attending conferences and retreats together or reading books by authors we both enjoy. And when either of us are experiencing pain or discouragement, we depend greatly on the other for emotional and spiritual support.

In our way of thinking, spirituality isn't a separate department of life. Spiritual intimacy isn't achieved simply by doing things that are "spiritual." Instead, spirituality involves all of us and everything we do. Spiritual intimacy is really a by-product of intimacy in other areas of our marriage. Put another way, the quality of our marriage dictates the quality of our spiritual lives together.

WAYNE AND MARCI RICE

❧ Your Turn

- Can you sense that God is rejoicing over you and your marriage? How do you, as a couple, join in his celebration of you?
- How is your marital maturity tied to your spiritual development? Can you separate the two? Why or why not?
- Talk about the meaning of your wedding anniversary. How do you like to mark this important milestone?
- What are the signs in your relationship right now that indicate you and your partner are on your way to becoming lifelong soul mates?
- In your mind's eye, what will your fiftieth wedding anniversary look like? What emotions will you be experiencing? What will you be most thankful for?

❧ Soul to Soul

To deepen your spiritual intimacy this next week, make note of:

- What you gained from this session together.
- A pressure point in your partner's upcoming week you will pray about.
- A concrete kindness you can offer your partner this week.

❧ Prayer

God of peace, sanctify us through and through. Fill our whole spirit, soul, and body with a rich love and keep our marriage securely planted in the person of Christ. It is in your faithful hands we entrust our marriage and ask for a lifetime of happiness and mutual helpfulness. Amen.

Biographies of Real-Life Soul Mates

Dan and Rebecca Allender grew up in the same hometown, began dating in college, and have been married for nineteen years. They have three children; Anna, 15; Amanda, 11; and Andrew, 7; and an Australian terrier named Maggie. As a family they love skiing, fly-fishing, and tennis. Their home is in Littleton, Colorado, where Becky is a full-time mom, wife, friend, and prayer warrior. Dan is a professor in the Master of Arts in Biblical Counseling program at Colorado Christian University and travels extensively with his seminar ministry.

Leith and Charleen Anderson have known each other all of their lives. They grew up in New Jersey but have lived in Edina, Minnesota, for the past twenty years. The Andersons' four children are Jill, Greg, Brian, and Jeff. They minister at Wooddale Church of Eden Prairie, Minnesota, where Leith is senior pastor.

Myron and Esther Augsburger have been married over forty-four years, are the proud parents of three children, and grandparents of two granddaughters. After nearly fourteen years pastoring in the inner city of Washington, D.C., Myron is now professor of theology at Eastern Mennonite University, and Esther is a freelance sculptor. They live in Harrisonburg, Virginia.

Scott and Jill Bolinder have been married twenty-three years and live in Grand Rapids, Michigan. They have three teenagers. Jill is a first grade teacher's aid and Scott is publisher at Zondervan Publishing House.

Pat and Shirley Boone have been married forty-two years. Though Pat is a movie actor, television host, and successful recording artist, and though Shirley is a successful author in her own right, they are both most proud of their four married daughters and fifteen exemplary grandchildren.

Bill and Vonette Bright have been married forty-seven years and have two sons and three grandchildren. They are cofounders of Campus Crusade for Christ International, where Bill is president. They have written numerous books and articles and have received several honorary doctorates.

Stuart and Jill Briscoe have been married for thirty-seven years. They have three children (David, Judy, and Peter) and nine grandchildren. Stuart is senior pastor at Elmbrook Church in Brookfield, Wisconsin, and Jill serves as lay advisor to the women's ministry. They also minister via video- and audiotapes and have authored over sixty books.

Jim and Cathy Burns have been married twenty-one years. Jim is the president of the National Institute of Youth Ministry. Cathy is a busy "stay at home" mom and manages to teach Sunday school and women's Bible studies. They make their home in Dana Point, California with their three daughters: Christy, Rebecca, and Heidi.

Tony and Peggy Campolo have been married thirty-eight years. They have two grown children, Lisa and Bart, and two grandchildren. Tony is a motivational speaker and author and teaches at Eastern College. He is currently developing a missions organization which is active in Third World countries. Tony and Peggy reside in St. Davids, Pennsylvania.

Steve and Annie Chapman write, play, and sing songs that deal with all facets of family relationships. Their straightforward messages of hope and healing challenge Christians as well as nonbelievers to develop a healthier relationship with God and those around them. The Chapmans have produced numerous CD's and are the recipients of the coveted Dove Award. Steve and Annie were childhood friends in West Virginia, and they have made their home in Nashville, Tennessee, since their marriage in 1975. They have two children, Nathan and Heidi.

Michael Christensen and Rebecca Laird have been married ten years. They are both ordained ministers and the parents of two daughters, Rachel and Megan. They live in Madison, New Jersey.

Chap and Dee Clark are authors and speakers. They have been married fifteen years and have three children. Chap is chairman of the youth and family ministry department at Denver Seminary, and Dee is pursuing a master's degree in counseling.

Tim and Julie Clinton have been married fifteen years. Tim is a professional counselor and ordained minister. He currently serves as the executive vice president of The American Association of Christian Counselors. Julie is the executive director of the Liberty Godparent Home (a home for unwed mothers) in Lynchburg, Virginia. Tim and Julie have one daughter, Megan.

Gary and Julie Collins have been married more than forty years. Gary was a professor of psychology at Trinity Evangelical Divinity School for twenty years and has written more than forty books. He is currently the president of the American Association of Christian Counselors. Gary and Julie are the parents of two grown children.

Jim and Sally Conway have been married forty-one years. They have three married daughters and ten grandchildren. The Conways have pastored for thirty years, taught at Talbot Seminary, California, and been on radio and television. They are best known as the co-directors of Mid-Life Dimensions and as the authors of fourteen books, many of which focus on midlife crisis.

Bill and Gail Donahue have been married eight years and are the parents of a six-year-old boy. Gail is a homemaker, and Bill is pastor of adult education and leadership training at Willow Creek Community Church in South Barrington, Illinois.

Ted and Dorothy Engstrom are parents of three grown children, have five grandchildren, and live in Pasadena, California. Ted is the former president of Youth for Christ International and president emeritus of World Vision, where he served for over thirty years. He has also served as acting president of Azusa Pacific University. He is the author of over forty books.

Norm and Bobbie Evans are president and director of Pro Athletes Outreach, a leadership training organization for professional athletes and their families. They have been married thirty-four years and have two grown children. They live in Issaquah, Washington.

Paul and Gladys Faulkner have been married forty-three years and live in west Texas. They have four children and seven grandchildren. Gladys is a certified elementary teacher. Paul is president of Resources for Living and also holds the chair of marriage and family at Abilene Christian University.

Steve and Elaine Green have been married twenty years and are the proud parents of two children, Stephanie and Michael. Steve Green is the senior pastor of First Church of the Nazarene of Pasadena, California. Elaine gives leadership to the women's ministries and is involved in various teaching ministries within the church.

Gary and Jorie Gulbranson have been married twenty-three years and have two daughters. Gary is senior pastor of Westminster Chapel in Bellevue, Washington. Jorie has been a junior high school teacher. Both Gary and Jorie have published articles on various counseling issues. They enjoy golf, exploring new cities, and listening to and playing the saxophone and violin.

Jack and Anna Hayford met in college in 1952 and have been married forty-one years. They have four children and nine grandchildren. Jack is the senior pastor of The Church On the Way, the First Foursquare Church of Van Nuys, California. He has written numerous books and songs, including the widely sung "Majesty." Anna is a supportive partner who keeps her joy and sense of humor in the midst of a continually mushrooming ministry.

Stephen and Sharol Hayner have been married twenty-two years and are the parents of three children. They live in Madison, Wisconsin, where Steve is president of InterVarsity Christian Fellowship and Sharol is a teacher and musician.

Don and Robbie Joy have been married forty-seven years. With two sons and six full-grown grandchildren, they are also caring for aging parents. Robby has wrapped up forty years of public school elementary teaching, and Don is professor of human development and family studies at Asbury Seminary in Wilmore, Kentucky.

Jay and Janie Kesler have been married thirty-eight years and are the parents of three grown children: Terri, Laurie, and Bruce. They also have nine grandchildren. Dr. Kesler is president of Taylor University in Upland, Indiana, and Janie focuses on the responsibilities of a campus president's wife, as well as enjoying her grandchildren and varied interests. Dr. Kesler was president of Youth for Christ for twelve years prior to coming to Taylor in 1985.

Herbert and Grace Ketterman have been married for forty-five years. Their three grown children are all professionals in their own fields now, and have made Herbert and Grace the grandparents of four boys. For twenty-five years, Grace was the director of a facility for disturbed children. She is now in private practice as a pediatrician and child psychologist. She has written fourteen books, and she lectures all over the country. Herbert was a physician in family practice for thirty years and is now retired. They enjoy traveling and reading.

Robert and Jeanette Lauer have three grown children. Jeanette is the dean of the College of Arts and Sciences at U.S. International University. Robert is the minister of Christian education at La Jolla Presbyterian Church. They live in San Diego, California.

Fred and Florence Littauer have been married forty-three years and are the parents of three grown children. They have been in full-time ministry together for the last fifteen years. They have written over twenty-five books, some of the most popular being *After Every Wedding Comes a Marriage*, *Personality Plus*, and *Silver Boxes*. Their ministry base, CLASS Speakers, Inc., is in San Marcos, California, and they can be reached at 1-800-433-6633.

Louis and Melissa McBurney are the grandparents of Robyn McBurney and Dakota Meador. They live in Marble, Colorado, where they are therapists at Marble Retreat, a counseling center for clergy. They've been married thirty-four years and have three married children.

Mike and Harriet McManus have been married for thirty years and have three sons, ages 24 to 29. Mike is the author of *Marriage Savers: Helping Your Friends and Family Stay Married* and *Insuring Marriage: 25 Proven Ways to Prevent Divorce*. He is also the author of a *New York Times* nationally syndicated column titled "Ethics and Religion." He has produced six videos based on the *Marriage Savers* material, which are widely distributed through churches. Harriet is a homemaker. They enjoy swimming and golf in their spare time.

Mark and Lisa McMinn have been married sixteen years and have three children: Danielle, Sarah, and Anna. Mark is professor of psychology at Wheaton College, and Lisa is assistant professor of sociology at Trinity International University.

Mark and Heidi Mittelberg live in the suburbs of Chicago with their daughter, Emma Jean, and son, Matthew. Mark is the Associate Director of the Willow Creek Association and coauthor of the book and the training course entitled, *Becoming a Contagious Christian*. Heidi has a background in teaching, which she uses to help direct a private Christian school. She also serves as a vocalist at Willow Creek Community Church.

Leslie Sr. and Lora Lee Parrott have been married for more than fifty years. Between them they have written more than a score of books, pastored a large church, and served as college president for twenty-one years. They are the parents of three sons: a pastor, Richard; a college president, Roger; and a clinical psychologist, Les III. They make their home in Portland, Oregon.

Ken and Joyce Prettol have been married for twenty-six years and have three children; Jennifer, 21; Toby, 18; and Luke, 12. Ken and Joyce have worked with Wycliffe Bible Translators for twenty-three years, first as translators in Bolivia, South America, and now as administrators in the Philippines. They have enjoyed the opportunity to travel and experience other cultures together as a family.

Wayne and Marci Rice have been married twenty-nine years and are the parents of Nathan, Amber, and Corey. Wayne and Marci live in Lakeside, California, and conduct "Understanding Your Teenager" seminars for parents of teens and preteens.

Duffy and Maggie Robbins have been married for twenty-two years. They have two teenage daughters, Erin and Katie, who help to make their home a place of love, laughter, and adventure. Duffy teaches youth ministry at Eastern College in St. Davids, Pennsylvania. Maggie serves as a full-time mom and has an active ministry discipling young women.

Doug and Catherine Rosenau have been married ten years. Doug is the thankful stepdad of Catherine's daughter, Merrill. In Atlanta, Georgia, where the Rosenaus live, Doug is a psychologist and author, and Catherine is an interior designer.

Randy and Nancy Rowland have been married twelve years and have two children ages nine and four. Randy is the senior pastor at Church at the Center, an innovative Presbyterian church near the Space Needle in Seattle, Washington. He has a Master of Divinity and a Doctor of Ministry from Fuller Theological Seminary in Pasadena, California. He is the author of *Get a Life*. Nancy has her Master of Arts in Theology from Fuller Theological Seminary. They enjoy boating, movies, and special times with friends.

Denny and Marilyn Rydberg have been married fifteen years and are the parents of four children. Denny is president of Young Life, and they live in Colorado Springs. Previously, Denny and Marilyn shared the position of directors of university ministries at University Presbyterian Church in Seattle, Washington.

Robert and Arvella Schuller were married in 1950. They have five children and seventeen grandchildren. Robert has pioneered innovative ways to reach people all around the world with messages of strength and hope, from the first drive-in church in Garden Grove to the all-glass Crystal Cathedral. He has received numerous honorary degrees and awards from around the world, and at age sixty-eight continues to dream of new ways of communicating God's love.

Ronald and Arbutus Sider have been married thirty-four years and are the parents of three children. Arbutus is a family therapist, and Ron is president of Evangelicals for Social Action and professor of theology and culture at Eastern Baptist Theological Seminary.

Chuck and Barb Snyder have been married forty years and have three children and six grandchildren. Chuck and Barb do marriage seminars around the country based on their book called *Incompatibility: Grounds for a Great Marriage*. Chuck's latest book is called *Men: Some Assembly Required*. They serve on the associate staff of Pro Athletes Outreach and do personal and marriage counseling for professional athletes nationwide.

Pat and Joyce Springle have been married for eighteen years and are the parents of Catherine, 14 and Taylor, 13. Pat is the president of Baxter Press in Friendswood, Texas, and the author of several books on emotional and spiritual health.

David and Jan Stoop have been married for thirty-eight years and have three married sons and three grandchildren. Dr. Stoop is a clinical psychologist and the associate dean of the Graduate School of Psychology at Fuller Theological Seminary. He is also the founder and co-director of the Center for Family Therapy. Jan is a doctoral candidate in psychology and spends a lot of time doing her favorite thing—being a grandmother. The Stoops have authored a number of books together. They enjoy leading marriage seminars and retreats. They live in Newport Beach, California.

John Michael and Viola Talbot are founders of the Brothers and Sisters of Charity at Little Portion Hermitage, an integrated monastic community of singles, couples, and families. As spiritual Father and Mother, they consider the community a spiritual family in Christ Jesus.

John and Barbi Townsend have been married seven years and are the parents of two children. John is a psychologist, author, and clinical co-director of Minirth Meier New Life Clinics West in Newport Beach, California. Barbi is a full-time mother and former elementary school teacher and administrator.

John and Cindy Trent have been married for sixteen years and live in Phoenix, Arizona, with their two children, Kari and Laura. John, a nationally known author and speaker, is the president of Encouraging Words, and Cindy is a retired elementary school teacher.

Charlie and Lucy Wedemeyer have been married twenty-nine years and are the parents of two grown children, Carri and Kale. Charlie, a victim of ALS, Lou Gehrig's disease, continues to coach football in Los Gatos, California, where Lucy is a real estate broker. They are the authors of *Charlie's Victory*, and they speak at home and abroad.

Jerry and Mary White have been married for thirty-seven years, are parents of four children, and grandparents of eight grandchildren. Jerry is president of the Navigators and an Air Force Reserve major general. Mary colabors in the Navigators and is a writer and public speaker.

Kirby and Ev Worthington have been blessed by their marriage and four adolescent children. Kirby has taught child and developmental psychology at various colleges and universities. Ev is a professor of counseling psychology at Virginia Commonwealth University in Richmond. Both write books and have recently labored over a book on parenting, which should be born in February 1996.

H. Norman and Joyce Wright have been married thirty-six years. They have two children: one living daughter and one profoundly mentally retarded son who died in 1990. Norm taught twenty years at Talbot and Biola graduate schools. He is now in private practice for marriage and family counseling. He has authored fifty books. Joyce is a homemaker who co-authored the book *I'll Love You Forever* with Norm. They live in Long Beach, California.

Zig Ziglar is the founder and chairman of the Zig Ziglar Corporation, whose mission is to make a difference in the personal, family, and business lives of people around the world. **Jean Ziglar** is a household executive who works closely with her husband in the writing of his books and daily newspaper column.